AIR VANGUARD 22

USN McDONNELL DOUGLAS F-4 PHANTOM II

PETER DAVIES

First published in Great Britain in 2016 by Osprey Publishing,
PO Box 883, Oxford, OX1 9PL, UK
PO Box 3985, New York, NY 10185-3985, USA
E-mail: info@ospreypublishing.com

Osprey Publishing, part of Bloomsbury Publishing Plc

A CIP catalog record for this book is available from the British Library

Print ISBN: 978 1 4728 0495 2
PDF ebook ISBN: 978 1 4728 0496 9
ePub ebook ISBN: 978 1 4728 0497 6

Index by Mark Swift
Typeset in Sabon
Originated by PDQ Media, Bungay, UK
Printed in China through World Print Ltd

16 17 18 19 20   10 9 8 7 6 5 4 3 2 1

Osprey Publishing supports the Woodland Trust, the UK's leading
woodland conservation charity. Between 2014 and 2018 our donations
are being spent on their Centenary Woods project in the UK.

www.ospreypublishing.com

GLOSSARY

AAA	anti-aircraft artillery	FAC	forward air controller	RAT	ram air turbine
ACM	air combat maneuvering	GE	General Electric	RESCAP	rescue combat air patrol
AoA	angle of attack	IFF	identification, friend or foe	RHAW	radar homing and warning
AIM	air intercept missile (e.g AIM-7)	ILS	instrument landing system	RIO	radar intercept officer
BARCAP	barrier combat air patrol	INS	inertial navigation system	RNAS	Royal Naval Air Station
BDA	bomb damage assessment	INAS	integrated navigation-attack system	RWR	radar-warning receiver
BLC	boundary layer control	LANA	50th (L) Anniversary of Naval Aviation	SEAM	Sidewinder expanded acquisition mode
BLU	bomb, live unit			SLAR	side-looking airborne radar
CADC	central air data computer	LAU	launcher unit (e.g LAU-3)	SUU	suspension unit underwing
CAP	combat air patrol	LTV	Ling Temco Vought	TACAN	TACtical Aid to Navigation
CAS	close air support	MER	multiple ejection rack	TARCAP	target combat air patrol
CBU	cluster bomb unit	NACA	National Advisory Committee for Aeronautics	USMC	United States Marine Corps
CG	center of gravity			VF	USN fighter squadron
CW	continuous wave (radar)	NAS	Naval Air Station	VID	visual identification
DECM	defensive electronic countermeasures	OCU	Operational Conversion Unit	VPAF	Vietnamese People's Air Force
ECM	electronic countermeasures	QRA	quick-reaction alert		

CONTENTS

INTRODUCTION   4

DESIGN AND DEVELOPMENT   7
- Photo Nose
- J-Bird
- The British order

TECHNICAL SPECIFICATIONS   17
- Fuselage
- Wing
- Flight controls
- Engine

ARMAMENT   21
- USN Phantoms
- RAF/RN Phantoms

MAIN USN AND UK VARIANTS   26
- F-4A (F4H-1F)
- F-4B (F4H-1)
- QF-4B
- RF-4B
- F-4G
- F-4J
- F-4J(UK)
- F-4K (Phantom FG.1)
- F-4M (FGR.2)
- F-4N
- F-4S

OPERATIONAL HISTORY   36
- US Navy
- USMC Phantoms
- Royal Navy
- RAF

CONCLUSION   59

FURTHER READING   62

INDEX   64

USN McDONNELL DOUGLAS F-4 PHANTOM II

INTRODUCTION

Most of McDonnell's design efforts prior to the F4H Phantom II concentrated on naval fighters, beginning in 1945 with the FH-1 Phantom, the US Navy's first carrier-borne jet fighter and the company's first production aircraft. Although only 60 were produced and the aircraft was seriously under-powered by its two 1,365lb-thrust J30 engines, it led to the similar but larger F2H Banshee. Over 850 Banshees were produced until 1953, serving in the Korean War and pioneering the multi-role concept that became a defining characteristic of the F4H Phantom II when design work on the latter began in 1953. Herman Barkey, heading design teams for both projects, devised the F2H-3/4 radar-equipped night-fighter/bomber and the F2H-2P photo-reconnaissance versions.

The Banshee's commercial success established McDonnell as a naval fighter manufacturer to rival Grumman, but its next project, the F3H Demon, undermined that position. Demon's destiny was tied to the US Navy's choice of the Westinghouse J40 turbojet, scheduled to produce 10,500lb of

With 122 reconnaissance mission markings this F2H-2P Banshee (BuNo 125687) operated from airfield K-3 in South Korea with Marine unit VMJ-1 in September 1953 during the Korean War. Twelve years later the squadron returned to action as VMCJ-1 with the RF-4B Phantom II in South Vietnam. (USMC)

F3H-2N (F-3C) Demon BuNo 133550 with VF-151, part of CVW-15 from 1959 to 1964, seen here aboard USS *Coral Sea*. "Demon drivers" enjoyed excellent visibility from the cockpit and although the increased wing area of this variant and its J71 engine improved its performance the Navy wanted the more powerful J57 engine, used in its F-8 Crusader. The Demon's shortcomings were attributed partly to the pressures of the Korean War and the urgency in matching the unexpectedly high-performing MiG-15, causing over-hasty development of several fighter types. (USN)

afterburning thrust. This seemed adequate for a short-range fleet defense interceptor and McDonnell broke with its own twin-engine design norm in accepting a weight-saving, single J40. Changes in naval policy made its first supersonic fighter, the Douglas F4D Skyray, its principal interceptor, moving the F3H to the longer-range air superiority mission. This required extra fuel and the installation of an AN/APQ-50 search radar. Persistent delays and performance shortfalls with the J40 forced McDonnell to deliver the first 56 F3H-1N Demons with the inadequate J40-22 engine before being allowed to re-engine the aircraft with the 14,250lb thrust Allison J71. This new engine enabled 519 F3H-2N and -2Ms ("M" indicated Sparrow missile capability) to enter USN service from 1956 despite accidents and groundings, although the over-weight fighter never attained its intended supersonic performance. Twenty-one earlier F3H-1Ns were not re-engined and went straight from the factory to a maintenance training center, with 200 unwanted J40s.

Despite these problems, the F3H-2M version provided valuable experience of the AIM-7C Sparrow semi-active, beam-riding missile and its AN/APG-51A guidance radar, vital in the evolution of the Phantom II. The extensively revised Demon had a successful USN career between 1956 and 1964 which saved McDonnell's reputation. Fortunately, from May 1953 the company also had USAF orders for its F-101 Voodoo. Conceived as a long-range bomber escort and powered by the newly available J57 turbojet, the massive F-101 demonstrated the company's versatility when it was progressively developed into variants for nuclear strike, photo-reconnaissance and two-seat, all-weather interception.

Both supernatural offspring, Voodoo and Demon (McDonnell had reserved at the War Department any aircraft names originating in the spirit world), were visibly strong design influences on the next McDonnell fighter. Twin engines were reinstated partly because naval doctrine favored the over-water safety factor of a second engine. In 1953 the company began work on a twin-engine F3H derivative, the F3HG/H, hoping to capitalize on the proven

features of the Demon. It earned a speculative "letter of intent" from the Navy in September 1954 for a two-seat, all-weather attack aircraft with four 20mm guns. It was the first McDonnell attack design and an indication that the USN wanted McDonnell to produce further innovative naval designs. Acknowledging the company's alacrity in seeking contracts, the Navy chose the F3H-G/H as winner of a June 1954 competition for an all-weather, two-seat attacker, assigned to the Navy's attack aircraft branch as the AH-1.

Although the F3H-G/H (seen here as a mock-up) was a vital evolutionary stage in the Phantom's development, McDonnell's chief aerodynamicist David S. Lewis realized that more major changes would be required when the USN specified the J79 engine and a new fighter mission as the F4H-1. Art Lambert and George Graff were tasked with designing a substantially new airframe. (McDonnell Douglas)

Officers at that branch were working towards a specification leading to the heavier A-5 Vigilante and they considered the AH-1 too small. It was therefore passed back to the fighter branch in December 1954 as it appeared to be "designed along the all-weather general purpose fighter lines." However, the concept took with it attack characteristics, notably 11 ordnance pylon hard-points, that would become crucial elements in the design's later life when nine of them were retained for use in the production Phantom II. Herman Barkey and chief aerodynamicist David Lewis worked on two single-seat versions; the F3H-G using the J65 (British Sapphire) engine and the F3H-H with the General Electric J79, sponsored by the USAF for its F-104 Starfighter and B-58 Hustler. The Navy expressed cautious interest.

The advent of Forrestal-class super-carriers in 1954 allowed McDonnell to enlarge the F3H-G/H into a multi-mission aircraft for these bigger aircraft carriers. The designers also proposed separate nose modules configured for 20mm guns, reconnaissance, ECM equipment or air-to-ground rockets which would be interchanged, depending on the day's mission requirements. Two-seat noses were proposed for air-strike co-ordination or training. The difficulties in reconfiguring aircraft in the cramped, under-deck hangars and resolving aircraft center of gravity (CG) differences compelled cancelation of this plan by June 1955.

When fighter branch representatives inspected the AH-1 mock-up in April 1955 they affirmed that the Navy now wanted a long-range fleet defense fighter, the F4H-1. It would patrol for up to three hours, dashing at supersonic speed to intercept intruders far from the carrier. McDonnell had already anticipated that this mission would require two crewmen, guided missiles and twin afterburning engines. The threat of Soviet bombers attacking the fleet from 50,000ft (beyond the reach of existing naval fighters with guns and free-flight rocket armament) would be met by radar-guided missiles that would effectively extend the fighter's interception altitude. From June 1956 the Sparrow III became the F4H-1's primary armament, although the fighter's wing had previously been strengthened to withstand the forces of a supersonic "snap up" climb to launch free-flight rockets. In April 1957 the 20mm cannon were deleted since Sidewinders became the secondary weapon and the Raytheon Aero X1A radar fire-control system became a missiles-only system.

It would be another decade before internal gun armament was approved for a Phantom variant.

Although much of the design detail was still to be settled, McDonnell received a contract for seven F4H-1 prototypes in July 1955, stipulating the standard 30-month period up to a first flight. The evolution of a twin-engine F3H into a completely new design that became America's most important postwar fighter took on new urgency and occupied McDonnell's best engineers.

DESIGN AND DEVELOPMENT

Instability at high speeds was a major problem for early supersonic fighters and McDonnell designers devoted much effort to preventing it. Wind-tunnel tests showed that the F4H-1's wing could have the F3H's sweep-back angle but it had to be thinner to attain the required speed. The tail was raised to clear the fierce heat of two afterburning J79s and its underside was clad in titanium, an innovative metal at the time. The risk of supersonic pitch-up was reduced by extending the leading edge of the outboard wing forward by four inches and the NACA (National Advisory Committee for Aeronautics)-developed technique of area-ruling the fuselage reduced transonic buffeting. Danger of "roll coupling" (uncontrollable supersonic oscillations in roll and yaw during a turn) required an automatic stability augmentation system to harmonize the pilot's control inputs. Its vertical tail, partially constructed from a weight-saving honeycomb sandwich structure, was much larger than the F3H's for adequate supersonic directional stability. It was also found that a slight wing dihedral improved roll stability. The flat, low-mounted wing of the F3H-G/H with its lengthy main spar gave a slight anhedral, resolved by angling the folding outer portions upwards by 12 degrees to give a slight overall dihedral. Also, the one-piece horizontal tail (or stabilator) was angled downwards at 23 degrees.

Developing and equipping the aircraft was accomplished under the USN's recently introduced weapons systems concept, encompassing the airframe and all its equipment. Allowing the principal manufacturer more control over choosing and supervising sub-contractors was seen as a way of improving efficiency in delivering new aircraft. However, many major systems including engines, missiles, the Lear AJB-3 bombing system and the radar were contracted by the USN as government-furnished equipment (GFE) for use in several aircraft types. Standardization rules also applied to cockpit equipment, although McDonnell decided on the innovative AiResearch central air data computer (CADC) which managed all the information for the aircrew, and the Stanley ejection seats – which the Navy later replaced with slightly heavier,

The first F4H-1, BuNo 142259, was effectively a single-seater. Hand-built alongside McDonnell's Demon production line it had J79-GE-2 engines developing 16,500lb thrust, early intake configuration and a pointed (but ballast-filled) nose for the 24in. AN/APQ-50 radar scanner. The downward-angled stabilator gave rise to rumors that the aircraft's tail had been trapped in the St Louis hangar doors. The prototype's brief but spectacular career ended after 254.5 flying hours when it crashed on October 21, 1959 during the final practice flight for Project *Top Flight*. (McDonnell via John Harty)

more costly Martin Baker Mk 5 seats for improved low-altitude safety.

The aircraft's principal mission, aerial interception with long-range Sparrow III missiles, cast the F4H-1 as a launching platform to destroy approaching bombers head-on long before they could hit USN ships. The priorities were high supersonic speed to meet the threat rapidly, powerful radar to detect the enemy and accurate guidance of the missiles that would extend the aircraft's hitting power and travel much faster than the F4H-1 itself. If a second attack at closer quarters was needed the Sidewinder, another USN-initiated project, could be used for a stern attack. The Raytheon Manufacturing Company began work on its Sparrow III missile in 1951, modifying an earlier Sparrow design to include a continuous-wave (CW) target seeker head. This semi-active system used the aircraft's search radar to find the approximate position of the target and pass the information to the Raytheon AN/APA-128 CW tracking system, which locked the radar antenna onto the target. The resulting radar returns from the target were then passed to the missile's CW seeker, enabling the missile to follow the radar beam to the target.

This method required the launch aircraft to keep its radar locked onto the target throughout the missile's flight. At long range, against a non-maneuvering target and with no immediate threats to the launch aircraft, that posed few problems. In fact, the majority of actual interceptions by Sparrow-firing Phantoms would take place in very different combat environments. The design of the Sparrow III allowed for Mach 2 launching so McDonnell incorporated four recesses into the lower fuselage for the missiles, including all but their two lower guidance fins, to reduce drag to insignificant levels and maintain Mach 2 speed. Each recess had an ejector to kick the missile free of the aircraft's boundary layer air, preventing rocket exhaust damage to the fuselage.

Westinghouse's AN/APQ-50, used in the F4D Skyray, was the selected radar. It was improved by moving its component modules, dispersed around previous user airframes, into a single, cylindrical container that would fit into the nose of the F4H-1 and slide out on a rail to ease maintenance. However, the F4H-1 prototype's radome was sized for a 24-inch diameter antenna for the Autonetics radar that the Navy had specified before the AN/APQ-50 was selected in 1956 and installed in the second YF4H-1 (BuNo142260). Westinghouse insisted that a 32-inch antenna was needed for the radar to achieve its optimum range and the USN agreed, renaming the system AN/APQ-72 with the larger antenna. A larger radome was therefore required and McDonnell engaged the Brunswick Company to produce the biggest one ever fitted to a fighter at the time. It was constructed from fiberglass and epoxy resin, carefully shaped to give radar-transparent surfaces and installed in the seventh (BuNo 143392) and subsequent aircraft.

Selecting the AIM-9B Sidewinder in April 1957 was partly inspired by its simplicity and reliability compared with the more complex and expensive AIM-7. Rejecting Raytheon's offer of a cut-price, heat-seeking Sparrow alternative, the USN elected to increase the Sidewinder's effectiveness by fitting an ACF Electronics AAA-4 infra-red/electro-magnetic seeker head in a 6-inch housing beneath the F4H-1's main radome. However, rapid advances in Sidewinder development soon made it redundant.

As insurance against another Demon disaster, the USN ordered two prototypes of an upgraded LTV F-8 Crusader, designated F8U-3 and powered by the massive J75 engine. With boundary layer control and Sparrow armament, the revised fighter included similar radar and fire-control systems to the F4H's. The September 1958 competitive fly-off trials between the first

YF4H-1 (which first flew on 27 May 1958) and the prototype XF8U-3 showed few differences between the two fighters in their primary interception role, but the two-seat, twin-engine configuration of the YF4H-1, favored by the Navy, won the day. The Phantom II's much greater ordnance-carrying potential was not considered during the competition but the XF8U-3's higher speed and better dog-fighting potential were considered less important than the Phantom's two-man weapons system management. If both had been ordered, as many recommended, the F8U-3 might have been an effective MiG rival during the Vietnam War.

McDonnell received a contract in February 1959 for 24 production-standard F4H-1s for an extensive Navy Preliminary Evaluation (NPE). Another 72 were ordered in September 1959, half with removable dual controls in the rear cockpit for instructional purposes. They had several innovations deriving from early tests. More powerful J79-GE-8 engines delivering 17,000lb of thrust replaced the J79-GE-2/2A or J79-GE-3A. From aircraft 19 (BuNo 146817) the cockpit was modified, raising both pilots' seats for improved visibility, particularly during carrier landings. The air intakes of the YF4H-1 were also straightened and a larger splitter plate was added. The 45 Phantoms following the two YF4H-1s were designated F4H-1F in 1961 (or F-4A, including the second prototype, after September 18, 1962) and subsequent examples became definitive F4H-1s, or F-4Bs in the 1962 designation method. Most F-4As had the Lear AJB-3A bombing system and General Electric ASA-32 analog autopilot and flight control system.

If the Phantom program had been terminated in mid-1962 the aircraft would still be remembered for the 15 spectacular World Records set by USN and USMC pilots between December 1959 and April 1962. NPE results indicated that the aircraft had exceeded its contract requirements by an overall 75 percent, in itself a record. The USN and McDonnell knew they could show off the new fighter's performance confidently to attract potential customers. Sadly, this began with the loss of the first YF4H-1 and company test pilot Gerald Huelsbeck during Project *Top Flight*, a first attempt at the World Altitude Record on October 21, 1959. The aircraft caught fire and disintegrated in a zoom climb above Mach 2 when an engine access door became detached. "Zeke" Huelsbeck was unable to eject from the wildly tumbling cockpit section. Cdr Lawrence E. Flint took the stripped-down second prototype, with engines boosted by water injection, to a new World Altitude Record height of 98,557ft on December 6, 1959. The aircraft exceeded Mach 2.41 in its run-up to a 50-degree zoom climb, burning off much of its hi-visibility orange paint and distorting the windscreen side-panels. At the apex of its trajectory the engines were shut off to avoid overheating (the afterburners ran out of oxygen

VF-74 *Be-Devillers* was the first operational F4H-1 fleet squadron, converting from the F4D Skyray in July 1961. Twenty-two years later it traded its F-4S Phantoms for F-14A Tomcats. The non-standard gray rudder of early examples allowed space for the squadron decor. Although it was assigned to the Atlantic Fleet VF-74 made two combat cruises, in 1967 and 1973. The former gave the squadron only five days on station before a catastrophic fire forced USS *Forrestal* to return to port. (McDonnell via John Harty)

at 65,000ft) and the speed dropped to 45mph as Flint began a dive to 45,000ft where he could relight the J79s.

The second series of flights was aimed at the World Air Speed Record in September 1960. Lt Col Tom Miller, one of the first two USMC pilots to fly the F-4, flew BuNo 145311 over a 500km course hitting 1,216.76mph, 400mph faster than the previous record by an F-101 Voodoo. Miller kept his afterburners lit continuously for 25 minutes. He released his 600-gallon centerline fuel tank as he accelerated past Mach 1.6, enduring cockpit temperatures of 125°F. His engines flamed out on touch-down after the 15.9-minute dash over a triangular course. Cdr John Davis secured the 100km record 20 days later with a speed of 1,390.2mph in a sustained 3g turn. In May 1961 five Project LANA F4H-1s won the Bendix Trophy for a Transcontinental Speed Record, covering the 2,445.9 miles from Ontario Field California to New York in 2hrs 48 minutes at an average speed of 869mph. Shortly after this very public demonstration the USAF decided to order its own version of the F-4B, a decision which was reinforced by the US services' first view of the Phantom's formidable ordnance-carrying capacity during trials at the USMC base at Camp Lejeune.

More record flights followed, including the Project *Sageburner* flight which saw Lts "Hunt" Hardisty and Earl DeEsch powering over the desert at Mach 1.2 and altitudes below 125ft for 3km. Whereas the speed and altitude records showed potential enemies that their bombers were at severe risk, and LANA showed how quickly land-based Phantom IIs might be deployed to trouble spots, the bone-jarring *Sageburner* flight showed that a nuclear-armed, low-altitude Phantom would be hard to stop. Project *Skyburner* was aimed at an Absolute Speed Record and Lt Col Robert Robinson USMC in BuNo 142260 reached 1,700mph at the end of a run averaging 1,600mph. Soviet bomber pilots would have been impressed by Cdr George Ellis's Sustained Altitude Record flight on December 5, 1961 when he held 66,443ft over a 25km course from a Mach 2.2 run-up, 11,000ft above the previous record height. The final series of eight record flights concentrated on "Time to Climb" records in Project *High Jump* and the unspoken agenda was to show the Phantom II's outstanding potency as a point interceptor. BuNo 149449 reached 49,212ft in less than two minutes and on one flight it zoomed to 100,000ft.

After its first flight on March 25, 1961 the F-4B was produced on McDonnell's new, rolling assembly line. Twenty-nine were delivered to the USAF as F-110As. F-4Bs had J79-GE-8A/B engines and full operational equipment including two MAU-12 outer wing pylons for 370-gallon fuel tanks or bomb-racks and two LAU-17/A inboard pylons for Sidewinders together with triple ejection racks (TERs) for ordnance, or an extra pair of AIM-7 Sparrow IIIs. An Aero 27A centerline rack supported a 600-gallon drop tank or a multiple ejection bomb-rack (MER). The USAF's purchase in 1962 increased production to 30 Phantoms per month and the cost-saving idea of inter-service "commonality" of defense products, advocated by President J. F. Kennedy's Secretary of Defense, Robert S. McNamara, extended to a new sub-type, the RF-4B/C.

Photo Nose

Whereas the USAF's F-4C was effectively a naval F-4B, the reconnaissance versions of the Phantom II began as a USAF initiative. The USAF needed a replacement for its RF-101C Voodoo, offering more than basic photo-

The RF-4B became a vital component in the US Marines' air groups. RM 20 (BuNo 153107) trails its brake 'chute on return to Da Nang AB from another combat mission, one of many hazardous wartime sorties that contributed to its total of 5,500 flight hours on retirement. (Tailhook Association)

reconnaissance. Initially designated RF-110A in January 1961 the proposed aircraft benefited from McDonnell's belief in focusing all radar and fire-control avionics in the nose of the Phantom II, requiring only minor modifications to the rest of the airframe. Replacing the F-4B's radar nose with a 4ft 7in. extension allowed room for cameras and a newly developed light-weight AN/APQ-99 multi-mode navigation radar with a much smaller radar dish. Deletion of the Sparrow system created more space in the lower nose area for an AN/ALQ-102 sideways-looking radar and an AN/AAS-18 long-wave infra-red imaging set. Detail design work on the RF-4C began shortly after the F-4C agreement was signed. An RF-4C order was placed in April 1962 and the prototype flew on May 18, 1964.

Although the "commonality" policy favored reducing the cost of the sophisticated RF-4B by sharing the project, the US Navy was already committed to the RA-5C Vigilante and RF-8G Crusader for its reconnaissance. The Marines, active participants in the Phantom II from the outset, were interested but could not place an order until February 1963. An initial batch of 12 was requested, later extended to 36 production aircraft after the prototype RF-4B (BuNo151975) first flew on March 12, 1965. Most examples differed from the RF-4C externally in retaining the F-4B undercarriage, rather than the wider wheels and thickened inner wing of the RF-4C. It retained an in-flight refueling probe and had no rear-cockpit flight controls.

J-Bird

Work on the RF-4C coincided with development of the USAF's F-4D, an improved F-4C with better ground-attack capability and the Hughes AIM-4 Falcon, replacing the AIM-9 Sidewinder. F-4D deliveries began in March 1966, accelerated by Vietnam War requirements and two months later the US Navy's follow-on to the F-4B first flew. The F-4J incorporated some of the F-4D improvements including the heavier USAF main undercarriage with wider wheels (11.5 rather than 7.7 inches) as an inter-service spare parts economy. The wider, lower pressure (251psi rather than 350psi) tires were less expensive and better for landing on paved runways, a bonus for the Marines. They reduced blow-outs on landing although they were prone to aquaplaning on wet runways. Additional overall weight, which necessitated the stronger undercarriage, also prompted a new horizontal stabilizer with a slotted leading edge. This increased the stabilator's low speed aerodynamic efficiency for carrier launch and recovery.

F-4J-28-MC BuNo 153778 in VMFA-451 *Warlords'* version of the Bicentennial color scheme in 1976. The AN/AWG-10 pulse-Doppler radar gave the F-4J its main advantage over earlier F-4 variants. The radar transmitted at around 1,500 watts and its hydraulic antenna could be slewed 60 degrees in elevation and azimuth. The scan pattern could be gyro-stabilized regardless of the aircraft's attitude. Within a flight of F-4Js, each would cover a different search pattern and mode with at least one in "pulse" mode and others using pulse Doppler. (Author's Collection)

Also, the inboard leading-edge flaps were disabled to assist airflow over the stabilator and the ailerons could droop by 16.5 degrees with flaps and landing gear lowered, reducing the landing speed by about 12kts.

For the F-4J, Westinghouse developed the best air-to-air radar of its time, the AN/AWG-10 (Air Weapons, Guided-10) pulse-Doppler (PD) system, with the same mesh antenna as the AN/APQ-72, though this later gave way to a fiberglass version. In PD search mode it showed closing velocity with the target rather than range, detecting moving targets at up to 120nm based on the speed of the target relative to the F-4. At low altitude it rejected the ground returns which made conventional pulsed radars ineffective in that environment. The AN/AWG-10 was subsequently improved with digital components but it gave excellent target acquisition at the Phantom's optimum altitudes for air-to-air combat.

The F-4J entered service with VF-101 (which soon had 85 Phantoms on strength) for crew training in October 1966 and it followed the F-4B as the principal USN and USMC fighter-bomber in the Vietnam War. Numerous F-4Bs remained with both services and many of these went through refurbishment and updating from 1972, with reworked F-4Bs emerging as F-4Ns. From 1977, F-4Js were reissued as F-4S models, most of them with leading-edge wing slats to improve turn characteristics. Radar homing and warning (RHAW) updates were included in both programs, although fitting AN/APR-30 ECM to combat F-4Bs and RF-4Bs began in the mid-1960s. USMC F-4Js remained in Southeast Asia until the very end of hostilities and the Marines operated the F-4S until September 1992. For the Navy, transition to the F-14A Tomcat began in 1974 but several F-4 squadrons were still in business in the late 1980s.

 A

1: F-4B-28-MC BuNo 153915
VF-161 *Chargers*, USS *Midway* flown by Lt Pat Arwood and Lt James "Taco" Bell for their May 18, 1972 MiG kill.

2: F-4J-30-MC BuNo 153825
VF-92 *Silverkings*, CVW-9 (USS *Enterprise*), NAS Los Alamitos, November 1969.

3: F-4J-33-MC BuNo 155532
VF-33 *Tarsiers*, CVW-7 CAG, USS *Dwight D. Eisenhower*, May 1978.

4: F-4B-09-MC BuNo 149403
VMFA-122 *Crusaders*, Marine Air Group 11, Da Nang, South Vietnam, 1968.

1

2

3

4

The British order

Britain's Phantoms were the only export versions derived directly from the naval F-4B/J variants. The F4H-1's World Record flights from 1959 onwards enhanced its sales potential worldwide and McDonnell saw likely markets in aircraft carrier-operating nations such as Canada, Australia and France. Land-based Phantom variants were also seen as potential air defense fighters in those countries and in Germany, but the British Royal Navy seemed the most likely prospective buyer following the F-4B's European debut at the Paris Air Show (via RNAS Yeovilton, UK) in 1961 under the US military Project *Short Look*. McDonnell had already completed a project study of F4H-1 operations from British carriers in December 1959, noting that their smaller deck area would require additional engine power. Initial discussions between McDonnell and the Admiralty took place in April 1960 when the F4H-1 was proposed as a replacement for the naval Sea Vixen and Scimitar fighters. Most potential UK contenders had been cancelled after the 1957 Defence White Paper which advocated nuclear-based, missile-dependent policies. However, in order to sustain the British aircraft and engine manufacturers after these cuts, substantial UK participation in the manufacturing of an F4H-1 derivative was required. Further discussions took place with Rolls-Royce on the feasibility of using the RB-168 Spey (used in the Buccaneer S.2 bomber) to replace the J79 engine.

McDonnell also met senior RAF personnel in April 1960, proposing the Phantom as a replacement for the short-range BAC Lightning and aging Hunter, but four more years elapsed before real RAF interest was expressed. In July, a Royal Navy pilot, Cdr Chilton, flew an F4H-1 at St Louis and McDonnell continued to produce detailed studies of modifications for UK carrier-borne use. An F-4B with a nose-wheel leg that extended to 40 inches (twice that of the F-4B), giving an increased angle of attack (AoA) for take-off, was tested on USS *Forrestal* in 1963. Further progress was constrained by the UK's commitment to the Hawker P.1154 supersonic V/STOL fighter, nominated in 1963 as replacement for the Hunter and Sea Vixen. However, Royal Navy doubts about the P.1154's range, single-engine safety factor and long development span rekindled interest in a Spey-powered Phantom in October 1963. McDonnell had already proposed a Phantom powered by afterburning Spey 101 engines in 1962, forecasting improvements in fuel economy, maximum power and acceleration. This optimistic report foresaw no problems in adding afterburning to the engine and no need for substantial airframe redesign to accommodate Speys. Although Rolls-Royce would obviously benefit financially, the additional cost of the Spey-engined version reduced its sales potential for McDonnell compared with the J79 Phantom, so the UK government had to bear all relevant development costs.

McDonnell prioritized the RN Phantom project, basing it on the F-4J with its AN/AWG-10 pulse-Doppler radar, slotted stabilator, seventh internal fuel cell, strengthened main undercarriage with Type VIII tires, the "double extension" nose-wheel gear and antiskid brakes. By February 1964 cancelation of the naval P.1154 was advocated, leaving the Phantom as the obvious, cheaper alternative. On July 1, 1964 the RN Phantom program was approved and two YF-4K Spey development aircraft were ordered, making the UK the Phantom's first export customer. Meanwhile, the RAF was committed to the TSR.2 strike bomber to replace its Canberras but the Royal Navy's decision and the success of the F-4 in all three US services led to a re-examination of the P.1154 and the economies of sharing in the F-4 project.

When a Labour government was returned in 1964, proposing severe limitations on Britain's worldwide responsibilities and overall reduction of its defense industry, further cuts were inevitable. The RAF P.1154 was among them, ostensibly because of projected delays in its service entry date. An increase in the Phantom purchase (as a "major US–UK co-production effort") was announced instead. The HS.681 transport aircraft was another casualty but the widely anticipated cancelation of the TSR.2 in favor of the General Dynamics F-111K was delayed until April 1965.

On July 1, 1965 purchase of an initial batch of Royal Navy F-4K and RAF F-4M Phantoms was agreed, although the J79 vs Spey debate ran on until November owing to Spey cost overruns. In order to meet the UK Government's cost target, the Spey's high Mach performance had to be reduced by specifying cheaper metals for its turbine blades. Costs inevitably rose further when British firms tendered for parts of the "co-production effort" and factored in additional expense for research and tooling for comparatively small quantities of equipment to replace up to 50 percent of the F-4's mass produced US components. US Phantom airframe manufacture had been sub-contracted to 12 other companies, so this principle was extended to UK manufacturers. BAC (Preston Division) won contracts for the aft fuselage, fin and rudder, inboard wing leading edge and some engine access doors. Short Brothers and Harland made outer wing panels. Ferranti modified their TSR-2 inertial navigation system (INAS) to replace the US Litton version and collaborated with Westinghouse to license-build the AN/AWG-10 radar system, re-designated AN/AWG-11 for the F-4K and AN/AWG-12 for the F-4M. Martin Baker cartridge-operated Mk H5 ejection seats with standard USN harness were specified, later replaced by the Mk H7 with an under-seat rocket motor. Marconi Avionics, Cossor, EMI, Delaney Gallay, Dunlop, Goodyear and Hawker Siddeley were among the 45 UK companies who tendered successfully for components. Further work was anticipated from a similar deal on the GD F-111K, although this too was cancelled in January 1968 and its role was partially fulfilled by the F-4M. UK Phantom program cost estimates almost doubled between February 1964 and May 1965, seriously undermining the financial pretexts on which the aircraft had been ordered. British firms received no additional contracts for US Phantom work and numerous delays meant that the F-4K's service entry date was no earlier than the P.1154's.

While the F-4K was developed in parallel with the F-4J the RAF F-4M's timescale coincided with the USAF F-4E and it shared many of that version's

Phantom FG.1 XT 863/150 VL makes contact with RNAS Yeovilton's runway, displaying 767 Sqn's "Steel Chicken" or "Ten Ton Budgie" insignia. The F-4K/FG.1 essentially failed its first Naval Preliminary Evaluation in February 1967, mainly due to interface problems between the Spey engine and the airframe. Slack throttle control, unreliable afterburner operation, engine stagnation and flameouts were all encountered during the tests. A flameout required descent below 25,000ft and speed reduction below 250kts for a re-light. McDonnell argued that the engine was at fault while Rolls-Royce blamed the F-4K intake design. The UK Ministry of Technology's inadequately detailed specification for the engine was also a factor. (Author's Collection)

air-to-ground and air superiority roles. Both versions had the slotted stabilator, BLC (boundary layer control), a stronger arresting hook (stressed for 4.8G), TACAN (tactical air navigation system), and heavier-duty main landing gear. The extra power of the Spey 202s at 20,515lb thrust and the beefed-up undercarriage enabled the F-4K/M to use British-made ML ERU 119 bomb-racks stressed for three 1,000lb bombs, twice the load usually carried on the MB TER-9A triple ejector rack. Unlike F-4B/Js, the F-4K also had to be able to return to the carrier with weapons still aboard as an economy measure.

Of all the common modifications, installation of the twin-spool Spey turbofan engine with its greater mass airflow and larger diameter presented the most difficulties. Contrary to McDonnell's earlier optimistic estimates, extensive structural modifications were required including a new fuselage center section, redesigned engine bays and a 20 percent increase in the frontal area of the air intakes. The lower rear fuselage was deepened and the rear fuselage needed an extra 300lb of titanium heat-proofing. The drag-reducing benefit of the Phantom's area-ruled fuselage was partially lost and base drag beneath the fuselage markedly increased, while fuselage width increased by 6 inches without a compensating increase in wing area. The overall result was a decrease in maximum speed from the Mach 2.1 of the F-4J to Mach 1.94 for the F-4K/M, despite an engine thrust increase from 17,900lb to 20,000lb in afterburner giving almost 25 percent extra power. Performance was inferior to the F-4J's at altitude but slightly better in the low-altitude regime where most RAF operations were to be flown.

Extensive testing of intake configurations prolonged development time as McDonnell and Rolls-Royce engineers refined a series of installation mock-ups, seeking also to meet targets for engine removal for maintenance. The first production Spey Mk 201 was fitted to the first British Phantom, YF-4K1 (XT595) on March 19, 1966 for ground tests and it first flew with Joe Dobronski at the helm, on the scheduled date; June 27, 1966. It was joined on August 30 by XT596 and the two aircraft were dedicated essentially to lengthy engine trials. The first YF-4M flew on February 17, 1967, focused on systems and weapons trials. Initial engine problems included excessive idling rpm, unreliable throttle control and severe vibration in the afterburner combustion area at maximum settings. The fourth aircraft, XT858, was delivered to Rolls-Royce at Hucknall in July 1967 and three Project Transplant F-4Ks arrived at rain-soaked RNAS Yeovilton on April 29, 1968 for the RN's 700P Sqn, commissioned on April 30, 1968 under Cdr Tony Pearson, for acceptance trials, slowed by the 36-hour engine life of the available Speys.

The original Spey afterburner (essentially a bolt-on addition to a civilian engine design) took an unacceptable five seconds to light and even in production-standard Mk 202 engines it could not be lit above 43,000ft. Sustained afterburning was impossible above 51,000ft, well short of the target figures. Carrier qualification trials on USS *Coral Sea* in July/August 1968 revealed slow engine response times in the carrier-landing environment, which were eventually addressed in the definitive Mk 203 engine for the F-4K. More seriously, cracked turbine blades had been discovered in September 1967 owing to engine overheating at unexpectedly high power settings and cost-cutting in the choice of blade metals. USN flight clearance of the engine was delayed until March 1968, affecting the availability of modified "Blue Standard" engines in 1968 and "Red Standard'/Mk 202 engines until early 1969. Blade failures continued after service entry, delaying training schedules and prolonging engine maintenance periods with severe effects on aircraft availability until the mid-1970s. Despite all these politically induced difficulties the RAF and RN gained the most versatile and capable jet fighter that they had ever operated.

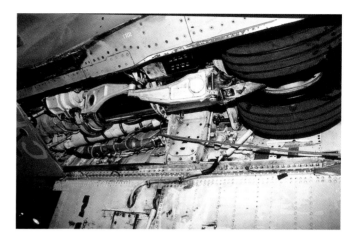

Landing gear retraction took three seconds. The pilot had visual confirmation of the wheels being safely stowed when a red light on the undercarriage handle went out and "barber's pole" position indicators in small windows on the instrument panel were replaced by the word "UP." The F-4 was the first fighter with a 360-degree steerable nose-wheel unit. (Author)

TECHNICAL SPECIFICATIONS

Fuselage

The F-4 had a strong, dense fuselage structure for the violent rigors of carrier-borne life. It was originally limited to 59ft in length to fit deck elevators on the Essex-class aircraft carriers but the majority of naval Phantom II operations took place on larger carriers. Aluminum was the principal metal, with a folding neoprene-covered fiberglass radome covering the radar antenna. A forward section, the most labor-intensive area, was split vertically so that all the complex wiring and ducting could be installed before the two half-shells were joined. Most of the space was taken by radar and avionics (or reconnaissance equipment for the RF-4B), the two cockpits, the No. 1 fuel cell, suspended from hangers, and the nose landing-gear well. The nose-gear leg extended by 20 inches for carrier launch. Twin, steerable wheels were held in place by a single locking nut.

An F-4J's sculpted main landing gear door. With the outer wing sections removed the wing fold hinges and the piping for the blown flaps are visible. (Author)

This forward section also included the air intakes, one of the most innovative features of the airframe. Long air inlets flanked the center fuselage, giving the aircraft its bulky profile and feeding the twin engines via an innovative variable-geometry air management system that avoided many of the engine-stalling problems that afflicted other fighters. The prototypes had fixed intake ramps but production aircraft had a large splitter plate located three inches from the fuselage to separate slow, boundary layer air. A second surface was hinged to the rear of the plate, with a slot between the two parts and 12,500 tiny holes in the rear section to bleed off low-energy air and eject it through louvers above and below the intake duct. This hinged surface extended into the intake area between 10 and 14 degrees to restrict the airflow at supersonic speeds, controlled automatically via the intake air temperature. Perforated nozzles in a "bell-mouth" ring ahead of each engine diverted a proportion of the air past the engine, preventing a stall-inducing air accumulation ahead of the compressors. This airflow cooled the engine bays and then mixed at the "convergent" nozzle stage with the air passing through the engine and into the "divergent" stage in the afterburner nozzle. It prevented the afterburner inferno from heat-damaging the rear fuselage.

The center-fuselage sub-assembly used various heat-resistant alloys, titanium and stainless steel to fabricate the engine compartments, separated by a central partition and enclosed by numerous structural and non-structural access doors. It contained five fuel cells (six for the F-4J). The rear fuselage section included the three-spar vertical fin and one-piece stabilator, constructed from titanium and stainless steel with honeycomb sandwich for the outer portions. Titanium skins with asbestos insulation comprised the keel area between the jet-pipes, which was cooled by ram air and covered with titanium shingles to resist the blazing afterburners which could heat the area beyond 1,050°C. A heavy duty arresting hook, stressed to 4.5G, was lowered by a pneumatic dashpot and hydraulically retracted. The extreme end of the fuselage included a 16ft-diameter ring-slot braking parachute compartment and a fuel dump mast.

Wing

The main wing section was a massive forging, spliced at the centerline. This torque-box was sealed to form a fuel tank and covered with weight-saving, tapered milled skins. A slight bulge above and below the inner wing, increasing local thickness by 2 inches on F-4J/S Phantoms, accommodated the thicker wheels. Another small raised fiberglass panel above the main landing gear strut covered the trunnion for the strengthened undercarriage leg of aircraft from late-production F-4Bs onwards. The outer wings on naval Phantoms were folded or extended hydraulically, reducing overall span to 27ft 7in. A small "beer can" indicator projected above the wing to show that the fold was unlocked. On May 10, 1966 an F-4B crewed by Greg Schwalbert and his "scope," Bill Wood, was positioned on USS *Franklin D.*

The slotted stabilator of an F-4J, also installed in some F-4Bs. The pivot point of the massive, one-piece stabilator unit can also be seen, also the small ridge-like projection below the tip of the stabilator. (Author)

Roosevelt's catapult and its wings were folded to allow another jet to pass on the crowded deck. When the pilot re-extended them they failed to lock and folded to the vertical position as the F-4B took to the air. Schwalbert continued his flight for 60 miles but diverted to Guantanamo Bay where he had to make a cautious 40 degree turn for the runway before landing at over 200kts. On their return, the crew received pairs of Wings of Gold insignia, with their tips appropriately "folded."

Pipes for the boundary layer control (BLC) ran inside the wing leading edge. This system drew bleed air from the 17th stage of the J79 compressor through a complex of pipes and directed it over the wing from ducts behind the leading-edge flaps when they were set in the "half" or "full down" position. Another set of slots appeared ahead of the trailing-edge flaps for air to pass over them when in the "full down" position. This laminar air delayed airflow separation over the wing, reducing turbulence and stalling speed and knocking 7kts off the F-4B's landing speed. Occasionally a BLC control valve did not close so that hot compressor air was trapped among hydraulic lines and wire bundles inside the wing. Rapid flap re-extension was then needed to avoid a fire. Flaps could be set at "half" to improve maneuverability in aerial combat, but prolonged use of BLC at this setting could scorch the flaps.

Flight controls

The stabilator and rudder were operated by traditional rod and cable runs, with a stall warning device to make the left rudder pedal vibrate. Rudder movement was integrated with the ailerons to facilitate turns at lower airspeeds and the ailerons were synchronized with single-piece spoilers that extended above the wing. Ailerons deflected downwards by 30 degrees, but upwards by only one degree and the spoilers rose to 45 degrees. When the pilot initiated a bank to the right, for example, by moving his control column in that direction the left aileron was lowered and the spoiler on the opposite wing was raised. At high AoA the rudder was used for turns, not ailerons. Flt Lt Jim Sawyer, the first RAF exchange pilot to fly the Phantom, found that "It is the only jet aircraft I know which, when under symmetrical power, depended so much on the use of

These traditional round dials would have been familiar to pilots of an early generation of jets, but later additions such as the HOTAS stick-top on this FGR.2 made the Phantom comparable with other late 1980s fighters. (Author)

With the engine removed the heat-resistant metals of the F-4J engine bay and the curved path of the air intake are revealed. The upper part of the bay is mainly titanium. (Author)

the rudder. I witnessed some very impressive inadvertent maneuvers by pilots who forgot this feature." Exceeding the maximum permitted angle of attack, particularly with ailerons in use, could make the aircraft depart from controlled flight and spin. If it entered a flat spin there was little chance of recovery.

Lowering the flaps also made the ailerons droop by 10 degrees without affecting their function. On take-off, leading-edge flaps were lowered by 60 degrees and trailing-edge flaps by 30 degrees, increasing to 60 degrees for landing. Hydraulic airbrakes below each wing were operated by a switch on the throttle control which opened or closed them in around three seconds, or stopped them at any desired position. Their effect was most obvious at high speeds. It was important to select "airbrakes in" before firing missiles from the inboard weapons pylons to avoid scorching the airbrake surface.

The flight controls were powered by two independent hydraulic power control systems: PC1 and PC2, one from each engine, working at 3,000psi. A third system, Utility, operated a range of other functions including the flaps, undercarriage, rudder, arresting hook, nose-wheel steering, refueling probe, and radar scanner. Loss of PC1 or PC2 through pump failure and low pressure for its 7 gallons of fluid could be handled by the other system, but a double failure usually led to crew having to eject. A Utility failure left the possibility of one-off emergency pneumatic operation of the refueling probe, flaps, landing gear, brakes, and drooped ailerons. Limited manual rudder control was still possible too. Pilot workload was considerably reduced by the use of an automatic flight control system (AFCS), giving stability augmentation in pitch, roll, and yaw, each with its own control switch. With the autopilot set to "Altitude Hold" the aircraft flew at a set altitude, taking data from the CADC and Lear AN/AJB-3 system. Gyros sensed any drift from stable flight and signaled the control surfaces to supply an appropriate opposing movement. For emergencies, a ram air turbine (RAT) extended from the upper left fuselage to power an emergency generator. RAT extension had to be triggered before pneumatic pressure dropped below 1,000psi.

Engine

The General Electric J79, one of the most successful turbojet designs, was manufactured for over 30 years and many remained in use for 60 years after the first bench-tests. A single-spool design, weighing around 3,850lb, the engine had a 17-stage compressor and innovative variable-angle stator vanes to direct the airflow with the aircraft at various angles of attack, reducing the risk of stalling. Naval J79s used an external air impingement starter system rather than the self-sufficient USAF cartridge starting method. In its final J79-GE-10B variant for the F-4S the prominent black smoke trail, which had made previous Phantoms visible for up to 20 miles particularly in humid conditions, was finally abated. Previously, using minimum afterburner on one engine, with the other engine at the idle setting, was the only way to reduce the signature trail. Variable external nozzles for the four-stage afterburner sections were hydraulically controlled to govern the speed of the jet efflux.

A Roll-Royce Spey 202. The engine proved to be very reliable without afterburner in the HS Buccaneer but many of its problems as the UK Phantom's power-plant arose from the difficulty in matching an afterburner to this turbofan engine. (Author)

The F-4J's J79-GE-10 had longer tail-pipes with only 16 nozzle "petals" rather than the 24 of earlier versions. Theoretically, the J79 could run for 30 minutes in afterburner below 30,000ft and two hours at higher altitude, given sufficient fuel. Excessive afterburner use "cooked" the drag-chute, stowed above the jet efflux, or over-heated and jammed the tailhook. However, in the opinion of USN MiG killer Guy Freeborn the engines were the Phantom's "biggest asset, particularly in situations where the aircraft's handling characteristics were pushed to the limits." In particular, its rapid acceleration without stalling was markedly superior to earlier turbojets. Inevitably, fuel consumption was always a dominant factor in combat as Capt Ken Baldry found: "The F-4 was an extreme gas hog, particularly at low altitudes in afterburner. We guessed the fuel flow at sea level in afterburner at about 80,000lb per hour. The 'low' light came on at about 2,500lb and it really meant it." The Spey-engined F-4K/M in full afterburner consumed 2,300lb of fuel every minute and endurance could be as short as 30 minutes. At maximum power all the fuel in two wing-tanks would be consumed in around 2 minutes.

ARMAMENT

USN Phantoms

Raytheon AIM-7C Sparrow III. This was the 1962 re-designation of the AAM-N-6 beam-riding missile, used by the USN from 1958 and replaced by the

The motor of an AIM-7F ignites as it drops away from an F-4S Phantom. Launch limits were 2G for the forward-mounted missiles and 3G for those in the rear missile wells. (US Navy)

AIM-7D from 1959. The latter was the principal armament for USN F-4Bs but was gradually superseded by the **AIM-7E Sparrow IIIB** from 1963. There was a tendency towards cross-interference between CW illuminators in two F-4s operating on the same frequency, causing premature missile detonation. In 1969 as a result of Vietnam experience, the AIM-7E-2 "Dogfight" Sparrow, identifiable by black "L" markings on its fins, was introduced giving increased maneuverability and shorter minimum range. The later **AIM-7F** armed some F-4S Phantom IIs.

AIM-7C Sparrow III	
Dimensions	Length: 12ft, diameter: 8 in., span: 3ft 4in.
Weight	400lb
Cruise speed	Mach 3.5 plus
Range	up to 29 miles
Warhead	continuous rod with 60lb insert (HE) head

Ford/Raytheon AIM-9B Sidewinder. A re-designated AAM-N-7 Sidewinder 1A, this was the original secondary armament for F-4Bs. The **AIM-9D Sidewinder 1C** with infra-red alternative head (IRAH) was similar to the AIM-9B but with longer range and higher thrust from a Rocketdyne solid-propellant motor, an ogival anodized nose and a guidance control section cooled by nitrogen stored in the LAU-7 launch rail. Cooling was initiated before entering a threat situation, taking at least a minute before the missile could be used. Background heat sources such as the sun or ground heat could "distract" the missile and it could explode in a target's afterburner heat plume rather than impacting the aircraft. Missiles had to be fired separately as a second "ripple-fired" round would merely seek the first missile to be fired. AIM-9D was successful during Operation *Rolling Thunder*. The **AIM-9G**, introduced in 1968 and used during Operation *Linebacker*, added Sidewinder Expanded Acquisition Mode (SEAM) enabling it to be fired off-boresight. From 1973 the **AIM-9H** added a solid-state guidance control section. The USN version of the **AIM-9L**, used from 1978, was cooled by nitrogen. Its indium-antimony seeker gave it all-aspect capability. **AIM-9M**, from 1982, produced less smoke and was more effective in resisting infra-red countermeasures and background distractions.

AIM-9G	
Dimensions	Length: 9ft 5in., diameter: 5in., span: 24 in.
Weight	191.8lb including the 25lb warhead

Ordnance (typical): Mk 81 250lb low-drag general purpose (LDGP) bombs, or Mk 82 500lb LDGP bombs, or Mk 82R Mod 2 TP 500lb bomb with Mk 15 Snakeye retarding fins allowing bombing from 150ft at speeds above 500kts. Mk 81s ("Delta 1s" in USMC parlance, or "Snakes" when fitted with Mk 14 retarding tail "spades") had a lethal radius of around 800ft but Mk 83 1,000lb LDGP bombs were favored for their penetrating power. Larger bombs such as the 2,000lb Mk 84 were not usually used.

Mk-series **laser-guided bombs** with PAVE Way 1 BSU-22/B canard fins and BSU-12/B wings were trialed by F-4Js of VF-114 in the *Linebacker* period of the Vietnam War. M1A1 "daisy cutter" 36in. fuse extenders were often attached to Mk 81 and Mk 82 LDGPs to cause above-ground explosion of the weapon for missions such as flak suppression but penetration before exploding

A typical CAP missile complement of two AIM-7E-2 Sparrow IIIs in the rear missile wells and four AIM-9G Sidewinders with TERs on the inboard pylons. F-4J-35-MC BuNo 155800 NG100 was the triple MiG killer for Lt Randall Cunningham and Lt(JG) William Driscoll on May 10, 1972. (US Navy)

was possible by arming the tail fuse only. Mk 82s with electric air-burst fuses were often used for flak suppression. During the early stages of the Vietnam War USMC F-4s were often seen with World War II-vintage 125lb or 270lb fragmentation bombs and 750lb M117 high-drag bombs owing to shortages of Mk 81/82s.

Mk 77 Mod 4 or BLU-1-B-C, or BLU-27 **fire-bombs** (**napalm**) were used extensively by the USMC where they appeared as "Delta 9s" on ordnance lists. Delivery at altitudes as low as 100ft was preferred owing to the weapon's poor aerodynamics and consequent inaccuracy.

The **Mk 20 Rockeye II** was the USN version of the Mk 7 cluster-bomb dispenser which was also used for CBU-78 Gator and CBU-59 APAM munitions. Dropping 12 CBUs distributed 80,220 lethal explosive devices.

Rockets: 2.75in. folding-fin aircraft (FFAR) rockets could be fired from 19-tube treated paper LAU-3 or 7-tube LAU-32 launching pods, weighing 500lb or 250lb respectively when loaded. Above 500kts the frangible nose-cones on the pods tended to separate, creating a drag problem. Warheads included high explosive, fragmentation, shaped charge, or white phosphorus for target marking. The rockets covered a wide area and they could be ripple-fired at a distance or salvoed at closer quarters, but they could collide in a salvo. More accurate results were obtained from 5in. Zuni rockets in 2-tube LAU-33A/A or 4-tube LAU-10 launchers but these had to be fired above 1,500ft to avoid potential damage to the launch aircraft. The 56lb Zunis accelerated to Mach 1.4 and were often used for flak suppression.

Hughes Mk 4 Mod 0 HIPEG gun-pod. A 16.5ft long, 1,350lb pod contained a Mk 11 Mod 5 20mm rotary cannon with 750 rounds, firing at 6,000rpm. Used extensively by the USMC the weapon was effective for ground attack, with enough ammunition for five strafing passes, although it tended to jam. VMFA-122's armorers even rigged a three-pod configuration on F-4B BuNo 148378, re-christened as an "F-4V" for their commander, Lt Col Verdi who favored the gun-pod.

RAF/RN Phantoms

Missiles: The main missile armament for F-4K/Ms was the Raytheon **AIM-7E-2 Sparrow** together with **AIM-9D Sidewinder 1C** heat-seeking missiles. The

MATRA 155 68mm rocket pods, 540lb Mk 1 bombs (inert) and practice AIM-9G Sidewinders were typical ordnance loads for the Royal Navy's Phantom FG.1s, such as XT 871 of 892 Sqn. The squadron's "Omega" tail design, signifying the anticipated end of Fleet Air Arm fixed-wing flying, was devised by its first commander, Lt Cdr Brian Davies. When the squadron disbanded in 1978 its aircraft were dispersed to 43 and 111 Sqns, rather than forming a new RAF unit. (Author)

more reliable **AIM-7F** with digital components was a potential addition but the UK government chose to develop the **BAe Skyflash** instead in 1973. This was a version of the AIM-7E with a Marconi XJ521 monopulse seeker and revised Thorn-EMI active radar proximity and impact fuses. It had a faster warm-up time, improved performance against maneuvering targets at low altitudes and better resistance to electronic jamming. **AIM-9L** Sidewinders were introduced during the late 1980s.

Guns: RAF Phantoms (including the ex-RN FG.1s) used the **SUU-23/A (XM-25)** gun-pod for both air-to-air and air-to-ground training. It contained a six-barrel GAU-4/A 20mm rotary cannon firing at up to 6,000rpm and self-driven by explosive gasses generated during firing. There were 1,200 rounds contained at the rear of the pod. It needed a one-second tracking time to compute the required lead angle.

UK ordnance

RAF and RN Phantoms used **1,000lb Mk 10/Mk 20 and 540lb Mk 1/2 General Purpose Bombs (GPBs)** including versions with Hunting Engineering Type 117/118 retarded delivery tail-units, which could also be adapted for US bombs. Other stores included:

Hunting BL755 600lb cluster bomb holding 147 armor-piercing bomblets with shaped-charged warheads. This was used from 1972 and replaced in

WEAPONS

1: General Electric SUU-23/A gun-pod (UK)
2: Hughes Mk 4 HIPEG gun-pod
3: Raytheon/GD AIM-7E-2 Sparrow
4: Ford Aerospace/Raytheon AIM-9G Sidewinder
5: LAU-10 Zuni launcher
6: LAU-3/A rocket launcher
7: SUU-30A/B cluster bomb
8: Mk 20 Rockeye II cluster bomb
9: BLU-27A/B fire bomb
10: Mk 81 250lb GP bomb with M1A1 "daisy cutter" 18in. fuse extender
11: Mk 82 Mod 2 500lb bomb with Mk 15 Snakeye fins
12: EMI pod reconnaissance system (UK)
13: Hunting Engineering BL755 cluster bomb (UK)
14: Mk 10 1,000lb bomb (UK)
15: SNEB pod for 68mm Thomson Brandt Armaments rockets (UK)

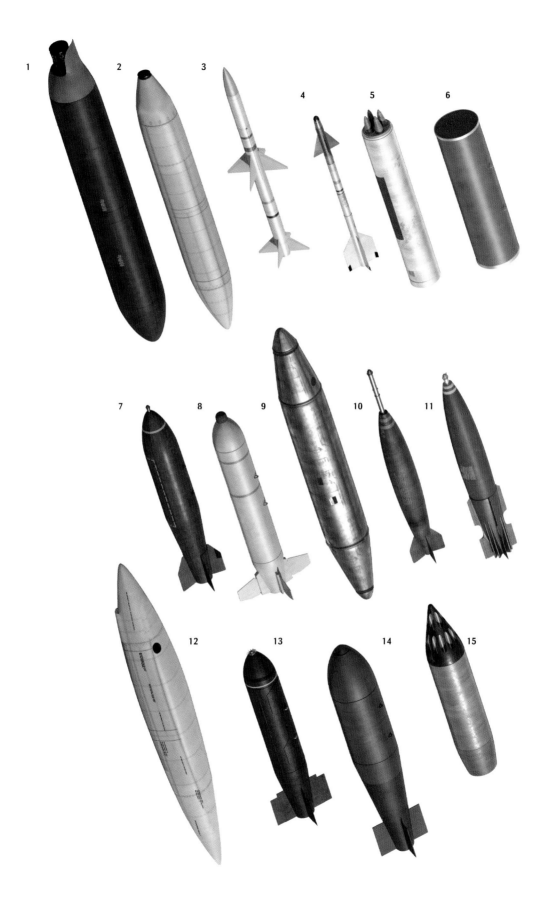

1978 by the Improved BL755, which could be dropped from lower altitudes. Eleven could be carried.

SNEB 68mm Type 25 and 68F18 unguided rockets in Matra F4 Type 155 18-tube launchers or Type 116 with 19 tubes. RN Phantoms used a similar Microcell rocket pod system.

Special weapons: Unlike most export Phantoms many UK Phantoms were wired for a single American B43 or B57 nuclear store on the centerline pylon.

EMI reconnaissance pod: As the UK government would not fund a Spey-powered RF-4 reconnaissance derivative, about 30 F-4Ms were adapted to carry the external EMI reconnaissance pod on the centerline pylon together with other ordnance for armed reconnaissance missions, although the forward Sparrows could not be used. The 2,300lb unit contained five cameras. A synchronized electronic flash unit in a modified wing tank was carried for night photography. Adapting technology developed for the TSR.2's reconnaissance pack, EMI and the Royal Radar Establishment produced two sideways-looking radar units for navigation and reconnaissance; an X-Band linescan, and a high-definition Type P391 Q-Band unit. The pod also housed a Texas Instruments RS-700 infra-red linescan unit. It was extensively tested from May 1970 to June 1971. Around 20 were delivered, 18 months late, for use by four squadrons (mainly No 2 Sqn) from December 1970 to mid-1977.

MAIN USN AND UK VARIANTS

F-4A (F4H-1F)

The 45 F-4As were built in five production blocks, of which the final two blocks (totaling 24 aircraft) were production-standard examples. They had the raised canopy outline, larger radar scanner and radome, revised intakes and AJB-3/3A bombing system. Aircraft from the first two production blocks (BuNos 142259–145317), with J79-GE-2/2A engines were used as test-beds and some received the airframe modifications made to Block 3–5 aircraft. Later examples (BuNos 146817–148275), of which the last five had J79-GE-8 engines, went to VF-101 *Grim Reapers* to begin training Atlantic Fleet crews, and VF-121 *Pacemakers*, under Cdr Pat Casey, at NAS Miramar for West Coast F-4 training. BuNo 148256 was VF-121's first F-4A on December 29, 1960. BuNo 145819, still with interim standard intakes, was the first Phantom II to visit Europe as a Naval Air Test Center participant at the 1961 Paris Air Show. Most F-4As were later used for ground instruction (BuNo 148260 was labeled TF-4A for this role) or fire-crew training.

F-4B (F4H-1)

The F4H-1 designation was resumed from Block 6 aircraft and changed to F-4B under the 1962 US re-designation scheme. Differences from the F4H-1F included the installation of fully operational radars and bombing systems together with the 17,000lb-thrust J79-GE-8A/B engines. Operational configuration allowed ordnance options ranging from four AIM-7s, four AIM-9s and a 600-gallon tank for combat air patrol (CAP) fighter missions to 12 Mk 82 bombs and two wing drop-tanks for USMC close air support (CAS) sorties. It had a single radio although crews would have preferred a second set. Updates during service included the "Shoehorn" AN/APR-30 RHAW fit in mid-1966, with a hook-shaped antenna under the AAA-4 fairing. This was replaced by the AN/APR-25 with a less prominent bulge covering its ALQ-51/100 antenna and no bulge when the AN/ALQ-126 system replaced AN/APR-25. On the tail-fin cap, the original AN/APR-24 RHAW antennas were replaced by two more prominent AN/APR-30 versions and then by a slightly different AN/ALQ-126 antenna. Slotted stabilators were installed in late-production F-4Bs and retro-fitted to others. The F-4B was the most numerous naval F-4 variant with 649 delivered to USN and USMC units following the first flight on March 25, 1961. Some remained in service until January 1978. One F-4B (BuNo 153070) was equipped as an **EF-4B** to perform electronic threat simulation for fleet defensive radar training with VAQ-33 at NAS Norfolk, Virginia.

The distinctive markings of VF-102 *Diamondbacks* on F4H-1 (F-4B-07-MC) BuNo 148402, fitted neatly on a carrier deck-lift. This jet was assigned to Lt Cdr E. T. Wooldridge who participated in early F4H-1 tests at Patuxent River and eventually became Assistant Director for Museum Operations at the National Air and Space Museum, Washington DC. (US Navy)

QF-4B

In 1970 the Naval Air Development Center at Warminster, Pennsylvania, began a program to convert 21 F-4Bs from production Blocks 6 to 11 into Full Scale Aerial Targets for air-to-air crew training. BuNo 148365 from Marine training squadron VMFAT-201 was the first. Ballast replaced radar, armament, communications, and autopilot equipment. Remote piloting was possible from the ground or from a DF-8A Crusader or DF-4J Phantom airborne controller. The aircraft had additional UHF command and control link antennas, a radar beacon and telemetry transmitters. These drones, conspicuous in International Orange paintwork, usually made several manned and unmanned flights as air combat targets, or for air-to-surface or surface-to-air missile trials before being shot down. QF-4B 149452 was the last to go, struck by an F/A-18A's AMRAAM missile on May 1, 1987.

RF-4B

This advanced day and night reconnaissance version performed similarly to the F-4B although its longer fuselage slightly reduced directional stability and its revised aerodynamics made it faster. Equipment included a Litton AN/ASN-48

inertial navigation system, a Texas Instruments AN/APQ-99 light-weight multi-mode radar offering very effective radar mapping, AN/ARC-105 HF radio, and the AN/ALQ-126 internal deceptive ECM system. The radar had terrain avoidance and terrain following (TFR) modes. It was possible to link the TFR to the autopilot for "hands off" flying but few pilots trusted this arrangement with its sudden "dive" and "climb" commands. The camera compartment housed an LS-58A mount for a forward-looking Chicago Aerial Industries KA-87 camera, which could be rotated

Built as an F-4B-14-MC, F-4G BuNo 150642 of VF-213 *Black Lions*, seen here in July 1966, had the AN/ASW-121 data-link modifications fitted to the ten F-4Gs carried by USS *Kitty Hawk*'s Air Wing for its October 1965–June 1966 wartime cruise. This aircraft reverted to F-4B status in October 1966, re-entering the conversion line for F-4N updates in 1974 for another ten years of squadron service. The dark paint scheme made little difference to the nocturnal visibility of the aircraft on deck as USS *Kitty Hawk*'s deck was kept totally dark until 1967 because of the risk of air attack. (McDonnell Douglas via John Harty)

to the vertical angle. A Fairchild KA-56 low-altitude scanning camera, or a tri-camera KS-87 array occupied the second space and Station 3 contained a KA-55A high-altitude panoramic camera (after December 1969) or a pair of large KS-87 split-vertical cameras. Other combinations were possible. The AN/AAS-18 long-wave infra-red imaging set included a recorder, receiver, and film magazine. A Goodyear AN/APQ-102 sideways-looking airborne radar (SLAR) occupied a space beneath the forward cockpit and produced radar maps from views to each side.

The AN/AAS-18 (monitored on a rear cockpit screen) was capable of detecting small heat signatures, such as jungle cooking fires, while the AN/APQ-102 could see moving targets such as trucks. For night photography, four photoflash ejectors in two bays above the jet-pipes released 26 M112 (each of 110 million candlepower) and 10 M123 (260 million candlepower) photoflash cartridges. An optical viewfinder enabled the pilot to view the terrain ahead at a 30-degree or 60-degree angle coverage through a lens above his instrument panel (giving a magnification of one-third or one-sixth respectively). Forty-six RF-4Bs were built, including 12 with the F-4J's heavier undercarriage and thicker inner wing. The last three (BuNos 157349–157351) also had the smoother, more rounded lower nose area of late-production RF-4Cs to reduce optical distortion caused by humidity around the transparency edges.

F-4G

In an attempt to emulate the USAF's comprehensive Semi-automatic Ground Environment (SAGE) system, in which interceptors were data-linked to ground monitors and could be guided without voice interchanges, the USN attempted a similar initiative for its fleet. Ships, early-warning radar aircraft, and fighters were linked, with control data passing through the fighter's autopilot and information on its position, fuel state, and weapons being automatically relayed to the carrier. It also allowed "hands off" carrier landings. Following tests of AN/ASW-13 data-link equipment in F-4A BuNo 148254, 12 F-4Bs were converted into F-4Gs from March 1963, using an expanded AN/ASW-21 data-link to work with a ship-borne AN/SPN-10 radar. The AN/SPN-10's signals were also returned from a retractable radar reflector ahead of the F-4G's nose-wheel bay enabling the aircraft to be landed automatically.

An approach power compensator system was also installed, fine-tuning the engine settings depending on the aircraft's AoA and flight control positions.

This "auto throttle" system proved popular: F-4G pilot Capt John Nash told the author, "I used these religiously; there's nothing better than being able to put both hands on the stick and have your airspeed stay the same." Ten F-4Gs were delivered to VF-96 in summer 1963 and then passed to VF-213 for USS *Kitty Hawk*'s combat cruise from October 19, 1965. In practice there was too much incompatibility between the advanced F-4G systems and those of the other aircraft and ships, so data-link was hardly used operationally. After the cruise the surviving F-4Gs were returned to F-4B configuration and seven were upgraded to F-4Ns. Elements of the system later appeared in the F-4J and in refined form in the F-14A Tomcat.

F-4J

Incorporating a slotted stabilator, drooped ailerons, heavier-duty undercarriage and AN/AWG-10 fire-control system with Doppler APG-59 radar, the F-4J was an improved but heavier F-4B. A seventh fuel cell was added to the rear fuselage, compensating for a reduction in the number one fuel cell's volume to accommodate extra equipment for the new fire-control system. F-4Js had uprated J79-GE-10 engines developing 17,900lb thrust. An AN/ASW-25A one-way data-link unit was included and the removal of the redundant AAA-4 seeker under the radome identified the F-4J visually from its predecessors, although a small DECM (defensive electronic countermeasures) fairing appeared in this position later. Command ejection allowed the pilot to initiate ejection of the rear seat, a facility that was omitted from the UK derivatives.

Modifications beginning in 1969 added AIM-9G Sidewinder Expanded Acquisition Mode and was followed by a helmet-mounted Honeywell AN/AVG-8 visual target acquisition system (VTAS) sight to enable the pilot to track and command missiles off-boresight by line-of-sight. It placed a gunsight monocle in the pilot's line-of-sight. Sensors on the helmet and around the cockpit coaming slaved the radar to the pilot's view. Cdr John "Hot Dog" Brickner explained that, "VTAS was one of those new systems that actually worked as advertised. Put the 'pipper' on the target and hit the nose-wheel steering button and, like magic, a radar lock. It was limited to the gimbal limits of the radar: plus or minus 60 degrees." Sanders AN/ALQ-126 deceptive ECM was added to later F-4Js, although the relevant wiring was covered by external ducting on the intakes owing to lack of internal space. One aircraft (BuNo 153084) became a **DF-4J** director aircraft for QF-4 drones at Point Mugu until 1985 and two (including 153084) became **EF-4J** target and threat simulator aircraft with VAQ-33. USMC squadrons began to receive F-4Js in 1967 and VMFA-334 Falcons gave the F-4J its USMC battle initiation in August 1968.

VMFA-333 *Shamrocks* made two cruises on USS *America*, the first USMC unit to join a USN Air Group, and two more from USS *Nimitz* in 1975–77. AJ 203 was an F-4J-31-MC (BuNo 153855), seen here with a combat ordnance load of Mk 82 low-drag bombs and AIM-9G missiles. (USMC)

Ten early F-4Js were converted for use by the Blue Angels demonstration team from 1969 to 1974. Their radars were removed and replaced with ballast, the automatic intake ramp movement was disabled as all demonstrations were subsonic and the gravity feed oil tank was modified to allow 30 seconds of inverted flight. Automatic flap operation was deactivated, afterburner settings were tweaked to allow minimum afterburner at 89 percent power and trim control was modified to give a constant 25lb pull force on the stick (reducing to 5lb at 500kts), increasing sensitivity for close-quarters maneuvering. The F-4J made an impressive air show participant but it required some strenuous effort by its pilots.

F-4J(UK)

Delays in the service introduction of the RAF's Tornado Mk 3 and the post-Falklands War requirement to maintain a defensive Phantom FGR.2 presence in the Falklands left a gap in the UK's F-4 force that was filled by the purchase of 15 surplus F-4Js for £33 million. The chosen examples had not been reworked to F-4S standard but still had substantial fatigue lives remaining. Nine came from the Aerospace Maintenance and Regeneration Center (AMARC) near Tucson, Arizona and others from Naval Air Rework Facility at NAS North Island, California. As the basis of the British F-4 versions, the F-4J had similar radar and required little adaptation. F-4J(UK)s retained J79 engines, USN avionics, formation strip lights and H7 seats and harness. The AN/ALQ-126 DECM was deactivated. Late in their six-year careers RAF H7A1/2 seats from Phantom FG.1s were installed. The aircraft demonstrated better high-altitude performance and reliability than the FG.1 and FGR.2, but the single squadron (No. 74) converted to FGR.2s, which became available after the closure of the RAF's Phantom OCU (operational conversion unit). Flt Lt Mark "Manners" Manwaring, who flew F-4J(UK)s and FGR.2s, commented:

> The F-4J(UK) had no ILS or INS (instrument landing system/inertial navigation system). It had two radio boxes which, unlike the FGR.2's, could be used at the same time. Not one switch in the back cockpit was the same as the FGR.2's. The F-4J's layout was easy to see. The RWR (radar warning receiver) was in a good position, not tucked away down on the left as in the FGR.2 but level with the navigator's face. Visibility from the back seat was properly thought out so that the only thing blocking the forward view was the front seat, with nothing else round the edges, unlike the FGR.2. The radar was superb. It had a Doppler spectrum processor rather than the FGR.2's Doppler spectrum analyser and all the connections were gold lined, giving a clearer picture. However, it wasn't updated for Skyflash missiles.

It had immediate afterburner re-lighting and more responsive engines but it lacked antiskid brakes (necessitating a cable arrestment on very wet runways) and it required the cumbersome Turbomeca Palouste external starting unit, which had to be pre-positioned for any excursions from the home airfield.

F-4J (FV)S

When the USN sought ways out of its commitment to the GD F-111B program early in 1965 McDonnell was asked for an alternative proposal, also using variable sweep wings and turbofan engines. The resulting design used the F-4J fuselage with two Rolls-Royce RB-168-27R turbofans and a new "wing glove" center section like the F-111's to contain the folded wing sections. The new outer wings would "swing" between 19 and 70 degrees and the stabilator, attached to an F-4J rear fuselage, was increased in area but without anhedral. Internal fuel capacity increased by 600 gallons and overall weight gains necessitated bigger main undercarriage wheels, housed in the lower fuselage. Improvements in all-round performance were anticipated and the design was offered to the RAF as the F-4M(FV)S in 1967 when the UK was still involved in the troubled F-111K program. By that time US policy had shifted from further F-4 developments towards a totally new air superiority fighter program. This evolved in 1968 into the VF-X (F-14 Tomcat) and, for McDonnell Douglas (the company name changed on April 28, 1967), the F-4N/S Phantom upgrade program and the F-X (F-15 Eagle).

F-4K (Phantom FG.1)

This was initially known as the F-4B(RN) and then F-4J(Spey) when the F-4J became the basis of the UK's Phantoms. A deeper rear fuselage, fitting tightly around the shorter, wider Spey engines, different jet exhausts and 20 percent larger intake area distinguished the F-4K visually. Four auxiliary air spill doors were added above and below the rear fuselage to expel excess bypass air at low speeds. Two modifications shortened the aircraft sufficiently to fit Royal Navy deck lifts. The fuel dump mast at the extreme rear end lost six inches and the scanner of the AWG-11 radar swung to the right, with its radome. Even so, the aircraft had little more than one foot of clearance at each end on the lift. Although the F-4K was ordered for the Royal Navy to equip squadrons aboard HMS *Victorious* and a refurbished HMS *Ark Royal*, fire damage to the former carrier caused its withdrawal and a new, larger carrier designated CVA-01 was cancelled in 1966 when the UK Government announced that naval fixed-wing aviation would be phased out. The £5m estimated costs for converting HMS *Eagle* for full F-4K operations were considered excessive, leaving *Ark Royal* as the only seaborne base and causing the transfer of 23 F-4Ks to an RAF air defense squadron.

Only 50 F-4Ks (FG.1s) plus two YF-4K development aircraft were purchased against an original projection of 200. With only 29 FG.1s the Royal Navy was able to equip just one operational squadron and a training unit. The reduced numbers inevitably pushed costs beyond the extra amounts already incurred by using Spey engines and other British equipment, including a Plessey PTR374 VHF/UHF radio, Dowty D403P UHF standby receiver, Hoffman TACAN and a Marconi AD470 UHF set. The Spey's extra power was necessary for RN deck operations, but maximum speed was reduced to Mach 1.9, and sustained flight at altitudes above 25,000ft required frequent use of afterburner. Ferry range was down by 490nm, strike range by 180nm and combat air patrol time was around 20 minutes below the target figures.

The Spey's extra thrust combined with the steeper angle of attack for a catapult launch using the 40-inch extension nose-wheel leg, required new 8ft high, water-cooled blast deflectors to prevent heat damage to the deck of HMS *Ark Royal*. The first launch from USS *Saratoga*, with the jet efflux blasting inches from its water-cooled deck-plates, had caused severe plate distortion and subsequent take-offs were without afterburner at reduced weight. Heat damage also occurred to the underside of the aircraft's stabilator.

Catapult launching involved a bridle attached to two "J" hooks beneath the wing root and the sliding "shoe" on the catapult track a frangible, dumbbell-

This underside view of an RAF FGR.2 in the RAF's air defense paint scheme shows the various reinforcing straps and patches that kept USN and UK Phantoms airworthy in their final years. (Dr Stefan Petersen via K. Darling)

shaped hold-back bar fixed to the deck and a strong-point under the rear fuselage. The bar broke under a strain of 95,000lb at full engine thrust, and the bridle was captured by a Van Zelm arrestor for several more "cat shots." A further refinement for RN aircraft was the Buccaneer-style Stick Positioning Device (SPD), a wire attached to the control column via a clutch exerting a force of 30lb on the stick to hold it in place on launch. It also counteracted the pilot's natural tendency to pull back the column under severe G forces, causing over-rotation, but it took time to set up and wasn't considered necessary by most pilots. A scale showing degrees of incidence was painted ahead of the stabilator to allow deck crew to tell the pilot the correct stabilator position for his catapult launch.

Towards the end of their time with 892 Sqn, F-4K/FG.1s, like their RAF counterparts, were fitted with the Marconi ARI.18228 radar warning receiver in a box-like fin cap. Its information was displayed on a screen in the rear cockpit and through aural signals. It provided the frequency band, scanning signature and bearing of radar threats but the Mk 1 eyeball remained the primary threat detector of hostile aircraft.

F-4M (FGR.2)

The RAF Phantom's designation included an "R" for reconnaissance as well as its "fighter/ground attack" functions. Unlike the F-4K (which prioritized air defense) it had an inertial navigation/attack system (INAS), long-range HF radio with a shunt antenna in the tail-fin in addition to the F-4K's Plessy UHF/VHF unit, a lead-computing gunsight, an internal battery, and a radar altimeter. Engine starting was by an internal starter which cut off when the engines reached 45 percent power. Early versions of the Ferranti INAS took 11 minutes to align while the aircraft remained static with its engines burning fuel – clearly a severe disadvantage for a 10-minute quick reaction alert (QRA) flight. Alignment time was reduced and the INAS matured into a system that deviated from course by no more than a mile after an hour's flight. Initially, the F-4M was also to have been carrier-capable but this requirement was deleted when the phase-out of Britain's carrier force was proposed in 1966 and it therefore lacked the 40-inch

C

1: F-4J-35-MC BuNo 155822
VMFA-232 *Red Devils*, MCAS Iwakuni, Japan, 1974.

2: PHANTOM FG.1 XT 864/R
No. 892 Sqn, Royal Navy, HMS *Ark Royal*. Assigned to Lt Cdr A. D. Auld and Flt Lt Alexander on the *Ark Royal*'s final cruise in 1978.

3: PHANTOM FGR.2 XV489/V
No. 92 Sqn, RAF Wildenrath, West Germany, March 1977.

4: PHANTOM FG.1 XV 571/A
Assigned to the commander of No. 43 Squadron, RAF Leuchars, 1987.

1

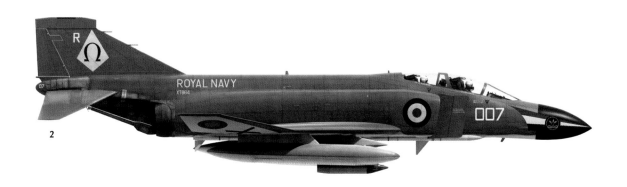

2

3

4

extending nose-wheel leg with two sets of torque links, the catapult spool "hooks" under the wings and the "quick-fold" radome and antenna. F-4M trials were delayed by incompatibility between the AN/AWG-12 and the Ferranti INAS. The first production INAS was not delivered to McDonnell until October 1968, 22 months after its intended date, but F-4M deliveries had already begun on August 23, 1968 when XT891 arrived at 228 OCU. The RAF removed wing-folding controls from the cockpit so that only one aircraft fitted into a hardened aircraft shelter (HAS) rather than the intended two.

F-4N

Wearing the restrained Bicentennial markings of VF-41 *Black Aces* in 1976 this smart F-4N-18-MC (BuNo 150456) was a MiG killer for Lt Cdr Jerry Houston and Lt Kevin Moore on May 6, 1972 in its previous guise as an F-4B-13-MC. At that time it had just been passed on to his squadron, VF-51, after a grueling combat tour with a USMC unit and Jerry Houston described it as an "over-the-hill rustbucket, one of the worst hangar queens I have ever seen." Even after extensive refurbishment his aircraft would bank to port every time he used the radio and it had been wired so that its Sidewinder "growl" tone blanked out all other radio communications. (Author's Collection)

Vietnam duties ate into the fatigue lives of the F-4B fleet by 1970. Cracks were occurring in wings and along fuselage centerlines. Delays and cuts in the F-14 Tomcat program also made the Navy re-evaluate the F-4B/S and devise a cost-effective life extension for its Phantoms. A major refurbishment program called Bee Line was set up at NAS North Island, California. The best 227 F-4B survivors were thoroughly inspected, rewired, partially rebuilt where necessary, and updated with some late-production F-4J features including a slotted stabilator, Sanders ALQ-126 DECM (with longer external waveguide fairings than the F-4J/S version), AN/AVG-8 VTAS, SEAM, a new mission computer, a 30kVA generator, and an AN/ASW-25A Link 4 one-way data-link. This enabled a controlling ship or aircraft to relay information to several aircraft at once, as long as their IFF (identification friend or foe) sets were switched on. Link 4 also offered automatic carrier-landing capability. AN/APX-76 air-to-air IFF was added, requiring an extra dipole antenna on the radar scanner. J79-GE-8 engines were retained and the cockpits were virtually unchanged. Life extension of up to 5,000 flight hours was anticipated. F-4Ns were reissued to squadrons from February 1973 and continued in service into the 1980s although 60 were converted into **QF-4N** drones from 1983. These aircraft were stripped to reduce weight and increase agility compared with the QF-4B.

F-4S

When Bee Line was completed a similar program was instated to rework 262 F-4Js as F-4Ss, although 47 "F-4J/S" aircraft did not receive leading-edge slats until later and a few never had them. Vietnam experience showed that Phantoms

faced an unexpected amount of close-in aerial fighting. USAF F-4Es had benefited in that respect from the installation of two-position wing leading-edge slats. Similar slats were devised for the F-4S, adding 1G to its turn performance and allowing deletion of BLC. It was tested on F-4J BuNo 153088, using a single slat on each leading edge. Re-plumbing hydraulics with stainless steel tubing and re-wiring with Kapton wire extended airframe life and hefty steel reinforcing straps were added beneath the wing spar and under the belly to combat fatigue. Smokeless J79-GE-10B engines at last abolished most of the aircraft's distinctive black trail and a digital AN/AWG-10B modernized the weapons control process. New dual UHF radios replaced the single radios of earlier Phantoms and electro-luminescent strip lights were installed for easier formation-keeping in poor visibility. The first F-4S took off from NARF North Island on July 22, 1977 and the first service example, albeit without slats, went to VMFA-451 in June 1978. The F-4S served with 25 USN and USMC units until the last squadron, VMFA-112, relinquished its Phantoms in 1992. It was popular with its crews. In Cdr Bruce Thorkelson's opinion the slats "gave the aircraft much improved nose control, especially at high AoA. This improvement was most noticeable during air combat engagements."

F-4S-23-MC BuNo155542 in the "lo-viz" markings of west coast USN Reserve unit VF-301 *Devil's Disciples* leads F-4J(UK) ZE 352 in 74 Sqn RAF decor. In its former life as F-4J-29-MC BuNo 153783 the latter had appeared in all-black decor as the famous XF-1 "Vandy 1/Black Bunny," complete with *Playboy* logo, of USN experimental squadron VX-4 *Evaluators* at NAS Point Mugu, California. (Jan Jacobs)

F-4 Dimensions (ft/in.) and Weights (lb)							
	Wingspan	Length	Height	Wing Area	Empty	Combat	Max Take-off
F-4B	38ft 5in.	58ft 3in.	16ft 3in.	530sq ft	28,000	38,500	54,600
F-4N	38ft 5in.	58ft 3in.	16ft 3in.	530sq ft	28,000	38,500	54,600
F-4J	38ft 5in.	58ft 3in.	16ft 3in.	530sq ft	30,770	41,399	59,000
F-4K	38ft 5in.	57ft 7in.	16ft 1in.	530sq ft	30,918	41,489	60,000 (runway)
F-4M	38ft 5in.	57ft 7in.	16ft 1in.	530sq ft	31,000	56,000	62,533
F-4S	38ft 5in.	58ft 3in.	16ft 3in.	530sq ft	31,000	41,400	59,000
RF-4B	38ft 5in.	62ft 11in.	16ft 5in.	530sq ft	31,200	39,773	54,800

F-4 Performance				
	Speed (mph, clean, sea level/48,000ft)	Combat ceiling (ft)	Combat radius (typical, miles)	Ferry range (Miles)
F-4B/N	845/1,485	62,000	420	2,300
F-4J/S	875/1,584	70,000	596	1,956
F-4K/M	900/	54,400	490	2,172
RF-4B	840/1,459	60,000	840	1,750
(N.B. Performance figures varied depending on external loads, climatic conditions, and mission requirements.)				

Blasting off USS *Independence*'s port catapult during her first combat cruise (June–November 1965) F-4B-19-MC BuNo 151478 AG211, in an early VF-84 *Jolly Rogers* color scheme, carries its bombs on outboard multiple ejection racks (MERs). Transferred to USMC squadron VMFA-122 *Crusaders*, this aircraft was brought down by heavy .50cal calibre gunfire while diving on a Viet Cong position near An Hoa on June 7, 1970, killing the pilot 1Lt Kurt Wilbrecht. (McDonnell Douglas)

OPERATIONAL HISTORY

US Navy

The first deployable fleet F-4B was BuNo 148365, delivered to VF-74 on July 8, 1961. Its final flight, as a QF-4B, was in 1974. VF-74 completed carrier qualifications on USS *Saratoga* in October 1961, progressing to the USS *Forrestal* in January 1962. Cdr Julian S. Lake, one of the Project LANA pilots, commanded the squadron as it emerged from training with VF-101. He sought to demonstrate the aircraft's versatility in air-to-air, air-to-ground missions and its primary long-range interception role. The radar and AIM-7C missile systems were honed in snap-up interceptions from low altitude and Cdr Lake's interception demonstrations against F-106A Delta Darts influenced the USAF purchase of the F-4C version. Another LANA pilot, "Scotty" Lamoureaux was Executive Officer for Lt Cdr Gerald O'Rourke's VF-101 *Grim Reapers* at NAS Key West as it trained the first 46 Atlantic Fleet F-4 crew members. Pilots mostly came from F4D Skyray or F3D Demon units, but Naval Flight Officer

D **F-4S**
F-4S-22-MC BuNo 153827 was built in 1967 as an F-4J-30-MC and converted to F-4S standard in January 1981. It was retired in April 1986. It is seen here in the markings of the Commander of Air Wing 5 (CVW-5), which had a 20-year association with the carrier USS *Midway* including two Vietnam War cruises. VF-151 *Vigilantes*, having made previous war cruises aboard USS *Coral Sea*, joined CVW-5 in April 1971 for two further combat cruises. In March 1986 the squadron made the last flight of an F-4 Phantom II from a carrier deck and it transitioned to the F/A-18 Hornet later that year. Aircraft NF 200 is seen here in the overall Gloss Light Gull Gray (FS 16440) color scheme adopted in the late 1970s. It has the AN/ALQ-126 DECM system, leading-edge maneuvering slats and formation-keeping strip lights added during the F-4S rework process.

(NFO, or RIO) "back seaters" were scarcer and this problem persisted throughout the 1960s. Some came from AEW aircraft like the EC-121K Super Constellations or Douglas AD-5Qs but others had to be trained on USMC TF-10B Skyknight radar-equipped fighters. Several F-10Bs had full AN/APQ-72 radars and F-4B radomes installed. Many former single-seat pilots found it hard to share cockpit duties with an NFO of equal or higher rank to themselves. Capt Fred Staudenmayer, a RIO who later commanded VF-33, commented, "Many a pilot wished the space was filled with fuel instead of a RIO."

Half the initial production batch of F-4Bs went to VF-114 *Aardvarks* at Miramar, the first West Coast "front line" squadron, which accompanied VF-111's F-8D Crusaders in CVW-11 for USS *Kitty Hawk*'s first cruise in September 1962. The *Aardvarks* made nine more cruises on *Kitty Hawk* up to 1975, including six Vietnam cruises, during which they claimed five enemy aircraft. As F-4B squadrons multiplied, some of them shared duties. VF-102 *Diamondbacks*, the second East Coast unit, flew alongside "day fighter" F-8s for two cruises. Specific operational techniques were soon established, including the preference for a 600-gallon centerline tank as it reduced maximum speed less than two wing-tanks. Pilots also adapted to the aircraft's nose-heavy characteristics, particularly at low catapult launch and deck-landing weights.

Aerial combat was still on the training agenda, as former F-8 pilot Capt Ken Baldry recalled:

In late 1963, as the fight in Vietnam heated up, people in VF-121 became concerned that it was not going to be a war where you launched missiles at targets over the horizon on radar. You were going to have to go in and see who you were shooting at. Visual identification (VID) meant that the people you were "VID-ing" could also identify you and engage at close range. This was a concept that the Phantom community found difficult as they had prioritized the Sparrow, a fine head-on weapon against a non-maneuvering target.

Several VF-121 pilots, including Ken and Peter Carroll, decided to

… see what the F-4B was really capable of and how best to fight the aircraft. We came to the conclusion that the F-4 really did best at low altitude and needed a lot of speed to be at its best. It had an amazing ability to accelerate when unloaded to zero G and turned at its best in the 450–500kts range. At lower speeds, being close aboard an adversary in the F-4 was no good deal because there was no gun, and throwing rocks was not really an option.

Ken Baldry's squadron, VF-96, was one of the first to prioritize aerial combat and he credited its 1966 commander, Cdr "Lefty" Schwartz, with this approach: "Lefty changed the face of Phantom flying to a very large degree." His pilots cleaned the stores off their aircraft to

… find out what the bird would do. Most of the pilots took to the idea like a duck to water and I cannot remember ever having more fun in an airplane than taking a clean F-4 out to the edge of the envelope and sometimes a bit beyond. Fortunately, it was a totally honest machine and would literally beat you to death in heavy buffet before it stalled.

McDonnell's policy of investing in heavy machine tools and building the early aircraft with hard production tooling meant that mass production could begin in 1959. Ten per month were rolling off the line by 1961, increasing to 30 after the USAF order was announced the following year. By mid-1964 around 320 F-4Bs had entered service with USN and USMC units. Fifteen USN squadrons flew them by the end of 1964, including two former Crusader squadrons, VF-33 *Tarsiers* and VF-84 *Jolly Rogers*. VF-154 and VF-32 transitioned in 1965 and this process continued until 1976 when VF-191 and VF-194 relinquished their F-8J Crusaders.

Joining battle

VF-96 *Fighting Falcons*, with F-8 unit VF-91 (later to convert to F-4Js as VF-194), was aboard one of the four US attack carriers in the Gulf of Tonkin in May 1963 during the Laotian crisis which took US warplanes to Thailand. The *Fighting Falcons* did not fly combat at that stage but former F3H Demon operators VF-142 *Ghostriders* and VF-143 *Pukin Dogs*, on their second USS *Constellation* cruise in 1964, participated in Operation *Pierce Arrow*. This was a punitive strike on PT-boat bases in North Vietnam on August 5 following their alleged attacks on the USS *Maddox* and USS *Turner Joy* off Vietnam. It was the first Phantom combat mission, followed by Congressional approval of the Gulf of Tonkin Resolution which opened the way for a prolonged conflict in which the USN F-4 squadrons were to make 84 war cruises. Navy F-4 crews downed 41 enemy aircraft during the war, losing only seven to MiGs.

Two *Flaming Dart* strikes on February 8 and 11, 1965 in response to Viet Cong attacks in South Vietnam involved four Target Combat Air Patrol (TARCAP) F-4Bs from VF-151 *Vigilantes* on USS *Coral Sea*. Three MiG-17s damaged an F-8D Crusader and evaded the TARCAP. VF-92 *Silver Kings* and VF-96 from USS *Ranger* took part in a second attack but from February 13, 1965 a much wider bombing campaign, Operation *Rolling Thunder*, was authorized. Cdr Bill Fraser's VF-96 also encountered MiG-17s on April 9, but they were Chinese Communist Shenyang J-5s (MiG-17F copies) and a chaotic 18-minute dogfight ensued close to China's Hainan Island as the F-4s lost flight integrity. At least 11 AIM-7 and AIM-9 missiles were fired but all failed, although one may have hit the F-4B (BuNo 151403) flown by Lt(JG) Terry Murphy and Ens. Ron Fegan. Their crashing aircraft could have been mistaken for a Shenyang J-5 and this was recorded (with much uncertainty) as a MiG kill for Murphy and Fegan. The incident was then swiftly buried by the White House. Several other "blue on blue" incidents occurred due to distant missile firing, but in some the targeted F-4 escaped merely because the missiles aboard the attacking F-4 failed. At least one Navy crew spent several years as prisoners of war after a "friendly" missile strike.

F-4B-15-Mc BuNo 151398 NL110, in the striking decor of VF-51 *Screaming Eagles* (popularly known as Supersonic Can-opener decor). Despite its combat-worn appearance, this Phantom remained in service until July 1977 after conversion to F-4N configuration. Assigned in this view to MiG killer Lt Winston "Mad Dog" Copeland (whose nickname adorns the fin cap) and Lt(JG) Dale Arends, it was flown by Lt Ken "Ragin Cajun" Cannon (his name is on the splitter plate) and Lt Roy "Bud" Morris for their May 10, 1972 MiG-17 shoot-down. Although speeds above 1,600mph were possible in new, clean F-4s, a battle-scarred F-4 in Vietnam would have had difficulty in exceeding 1,000mph. (R. Lock)

Most wartime Phantom combat involved attacks on ground targets. F-4B-26-MC BuNo 153019 of VF-213 *Black Lions* delivers its Mk 82 "slick" bombs in straight-and-level flight during a radar-guided TPQ-10 mission. This F-4B has the AN/APR-30 ECM additions to its fin cap and radome. On March 6, 1972, with VF-111 *Sundowners,* as *Old Nick 201* with Lt Garry Weigand and Lt(JG) Bill Freckleton in the cockpit, it shot down a MiG-17 with an AIM-9G missile. (US Navy)

Squadrons from *Coral Sea* and *Ranger* flew the first *Rolling Thunder* attacks and USS *Midway* with VF-21 *Freelancers* replaced *Ranger* from April 10. Like VF-96, this squadron had prioritized air combat maneuvering (ACM) in its training, which helped newly trained pilot Lt David Batson and his RIO Lt Cdr Rob Doremus when they participated in the first official F-4 MiG kills. After missile problems negated possible kills in the second F-4 scrap with MiG-17s on June 4, a VF-21 BARCAP (barrier combat air patrol) made a textbook, head-on Sparrow attack on four MiG-17s near Than Hoa on June 17. One fell to Cdr Lou Page and his expert RIO, Lt J. C. Smith. The other victim, as Dave Batson told the author, was hit by an AIM-7 that "swerved under the nose of the F-4. I lost sight of it but Rob saw it guide to a direct hit. I don't think he [the MiG pilot] ever saw me." Later evidence revealed that only one of the four MiGs returned to base after the victim's wingman ingested debris from the explosion. In 1997 Batson had his second kill confirmed.

The conflict widened and drew in other F-4 squadrons including occasional Atlantic Fleet units such as VF-84 *Jolly Rogers* with CVW-7 on the USS *Independence*'s only war cruise. Their experience epitomized that of most F-4 units during the war in that two-thirds of their missions involved flak suppression using 1,000lb bombs, armed reconnaissance or small-scale strikes with LAU-3/A or LAU-10/A Zuni rocket pods and 500lb bombs. As Lt Grover Erickson commented, "Flak suppression was a mission that I never anticipated as a fighter pilot and it certainly wasn't the best environment for the Phantom." By the end of 1965 ten F-4 squadrons had made war cruises in which their ability to carry twice the bomb-load of the Navy's principal striker, the A-4 Skyhawk, meant that they were often used to reinforce Alpha strike packages while the scarcer A-6A Intruders usually concentrated on precision night attacks. Later, very effective A-6A/F-4B daytime strikes were introduced.

Launching first because heavy ordnance increased their fuel consumption, six F-4Bs would head for the target within the package at around 300kts and 15–18,000ft. Over the coast their speed increased by 100kts and they led the attack against AAA sites or the main target, using their higher speed compared with the A-4 to evade the defenses. Ordnance was usually released at around 5,000ft from a 45 degree dive. Pilots in VF-41 *Black Aces* even practiced their own version of straight-and-level radar bombing using the AN/APQ-72 together with dead reckoning navigation. Many missions were also flown as

VF-114's F-4B-28-MC BuNo 153065 takes the wire on USS *Kitty Hawk* after another attack mission. The USAF's F-4C had an INS to enable it to deliver a nuclear weapon but the F-4B's bombing system was more basic, requiring aids like TPQ-10 or pathfinder aircraft in poor visibility. The AN/APQ-72 radar was the best of its kind, but the vacuum-tube technology of the day was sorely tested by humid climates and the forces encountered in aircraft-carrier operations. (US Navy)

pairs against smaller targets in South Vietnam, sometimes dropping CBU or napalm. The latter was removed from aircraft carriers after disastrous fires on USS *Forrestal* and USS *Enterprise*.

Escort missions for RF-8G and *Blue Tree* RA-5C reconnaissance flights, or OP-2E *Igloo White* sensor-dropping aircraft were also required and two F-4s were always on five-minute deck alert to counter airborne threats or respond to an emergency. Many carriers' crews were on flight duty for 12-hour periods. Like USAF Phantom crews, they flew night attacks on truck targets on the Ho Chi Minh trails, with only vertigo-inducing flares to help identify their targets. Ground-attack missions within range of the enemy's prodigious antiaircraft guns brought the highest number of F-4 casualties: 53 out of 71 combat losses. SA-2 SAMs accounted for another 13, and from 1966 to 1967 F-4Bs were retro-fitted with AN/ALE-29A chaff dispensers in upper fuselage compartments and AN/APR-26 RHAW threat warning receivers to counter this formidable threat. MiG killer Jerry Houston commented ironically, "The RHAW gear gave good early warning, but between the threat sector indicator, the flashing red lights and the high-pitched warbler, mostly they just accelerated your heartbeat." Capt Will Haff, on USS *Coral Sea*, had his own solution: "I always lightened my cockpit load by simply turning off all the things and equipment that bothered me. Unless on a vector from an airborne controller or PIRAZ (radar ship) I always shut down almost all electronics, including radar, while approaching the coast."

Because the F-4B's bombing computer was designed for nuclear toss-bombing, several squadrons (including VF-41, VF-114, and VF-96) devised jury-rigged manual bombing sights using an A-1 Skyraider sight in place of the normal Westinghouse fixed reflector sight-plate. Bombing techniques were usually left to each Air Wing to decide. Run-ins below 3,000ft to the target invited a welter of small-arms fire and a couple of bullets hitting the aircraft's unprotected hydraulics could soon incapacitate it. A favorite technique was to "pop up" from 4,000ft to 12,000ft and attack in a 30-degree dive, pulling out at around 2,000ft.

Operating from smaller Midway class carriers required careful weight management. F-4Bs from CVW-1 on USS *Franklin D. Roosevelt*'s only war cruise often deck-launched with 6,000lb of bombs and an empty 600-gallon tank which was filled as soon as the aircraft could meet up with a tanker aircraft. Landing on Midway carriers, with their short-span deck arresting gear, also required absolute minimum fuel to achieve the correct weight. This caused several F-4 losses through fuel starvation.

Whereas F-4s scored five MiGs in 1965 and none fell to "gun-fighting" F-8 Crusaders, the F-8 units downed five in 1966, mostly with AIM-9s, with only one credited to an F-4B. MiG sightings by Phantom crews in 1966 were unusual but 1967 brought major increases in Vietnamese People's Air Force (VPAF) activity as the air war closed in on Hanoi and MiG airfields. Nine MiGs fell to F-8 pilots later in the year while F-4B crews scored six, three of which were MiG-21s. Two of these were destroyed in an August 10 fight involving two F-4Bs of VF-142 *Ghostriders* during an attack on the Phu Ly trans-shipment area. Lt Guy Freeborn and Lt(JG) Robert Elliott in F-4B-22-MC BuNo 152247 were in the barrier combat air patrol (BARCAP) flight with Lt Cdrs Bob Davis and Gayle "Swede" Elie in BuNo 150431 *Dakota 210*. As Guy Freeborn described it, "We held station just under the cloud layer, instead of the normal 15,000–18,000ft, for the surprise element which worked just as we had planned."

They were kept informed of the MiG-21s' course and turned in behind them as they passed overhead at 22,000ft. Davis attempted to fire an AIM-7E but the rear left missile well's ejector cartridge was missing, preventing a launch. He switched the armament knob to HEAT and fired an AIM-9D, which went ballistic, followed by a second which missed but alerted the MiGs, making them enter a sharp turn. *Dakota 210* then climbed to get above the MiGs, leaving Freeborn to fire an AIM-9D that damaged the left MiG. Seconds later, Davis dived and fired two more Sidewinders, blowing away the MiG's rear section. Freeborn in *Dakota 202* went for the second MiG, firing two more AIM-9Ds (nine missiles were fired in all), one of which exploded fatally inside the target's jet-pipe.

Linebacking Phantoms

F-4Js entered service with VF-84 and VF-41 in February 1967 but VF-33 and VF-102 were the first to take them into combat when USS *America* entered the war with an East Coast Air Group. Capt Bill Knutson, who flew the first F-4J combat mission on May 31, 1968, found it to be, "heavier, but with the new stabilator and more responsive engines it was a dream. It was more stable

F-4J-35-MC BuNo 155787 is poised on USS *Constellation*'s catapult with its nose-gear extended for launching and a load of Mk 82 bombs and AIM-9G Sidewinders as its crew awaits the signal to engage afterburner. (US Navy)

than the F-4B and the extra engine thrust was great for ACM." VF-33's Lt Roy "Outlaw" Cash and Lt(JG) Ed "Killer" Kain achieved the type's first MiG kill, on July 10, 1968.

With the cessation of *Rolling Thunder* only one more MiG kill occurred before 1972 while F-4 operations were limited to South Vietnam or "protective reaction" reconnaissance escort flights. Lt Jerry Beaulier and Lt(JG) Steve Barkley of VF-142 were launched on Alert 5 aboard USS *Constellation* on March 28, 1970 to intercept two MiG-21s near Vinh. After a brief turning fight in which both sides fired missiles Beaulier in *Dakota 201* (BuNo 155875) hit one MiG-21 with two successive AIM-9s, reducing it to blazing wreckage. "The nose and canopy were visible in front of the fireball," Steve Barkley recalled. "We pulled up at the MiG's 4 o'clock and took a look as the doomed aircraft descended into the cloud below us." A MiG-17 was also downed by another crew (Lts Fred Vogt and Karl Volland) in *Taproom 112* but this was suppressed as the rules forbade engaging enemy aircraft unless they directly threatened US aircraft.

Jerry Beaulier attributed some of their success to his month of air-to-air training as one of the first students on the Top Gun (Naval Fighter Weapons School) course in March 1969. Bringing together the accumulated wisdom of VF-121 instructors, VX-4 *Evaluator* aircraft, and weapons development personnel and operational squadrons Top Gun produced a syllabus which, as double MiG killer Matt Connelly recalled, "taught us to fly the F-4 to its advantages and capitalize on the weaknesses of the enemy fighters." As Top Gun instructor John "Smash" Nash explained, "The F-4 was a superior ACM airplane, flown by the right guy. Doing ACM in the Phantom was more of an art than a science and some of the older guys weren't happy with flying the F-4 to the edge of the envelope." On return to their squadrons the selected Top Gun graduates passed on the knowledge to their colleagues.

The outcome of the new, aggressive philosophy was a long succession of MiG kills

In the markings of VF-143 *Puking Dogs* F-4J-38-MC BuNo 155889 has its left ALE-29 chaff dispenser open, AIM-9G and AIM-7E missiles uploaded and two Royal Jet 370-gallon drop-tanks. On November 22, 1969 this F-4J was lost while attacking a target on the Ho Chi Minh Trail. Loss of control, possibly due to AAA hits, forced Lts(JG) Herbert Wheeler and Henry Bedinger to eject over Laos. Bedinger was comparatively lucky in being captured since many aircrew who parachuted into Laos were never seen again. Wheeler was even more fortunate in being recovered by an HH-53 helicopter. (via Norman Taylor)

Lt Bob Hughes is congratulated on the MiG-21 kill which he and his RIO Lt(JG) Joe Cruz achieved on June 5, 1972 in F-4J-40-MC BuNo 157249 *Linfield 206*, one of two MiG-21s shot down by his squadron (VF-114 *Aardvarks*) in a single engagement that day. Hughes damaged another MiG-21 with his last AIM-9G but another Sidewinder from the F-4J-40-MC (BuNo 157245) of Lt Cdr Pete "Viper" Pettigrew and Lt(JG) Mike McCabe, struck it one second later and completed its destruction. Hughes, an acknowledged expert pilot, was killed in a January 1979 mid-air collision between an F-4J and a TA-4J Skyhawk which he was flying as an air combat maneuvering (ACM) adversary training pilot near San Diego, California. (US Navy)

F-4J-46-MC BuNo 158365 from the penultimate production batch cruises over the South China Sea in the summer of 1974. VF-21 *Freelancers* had a long association with the F-4 from late 1962 until November 1983. In December 1979 it was the first fleet unit to acquire the F-4S. (Jan Jacobs)

– 25 in 1972 and another near the end of the conflict in 1973 – in which Top Gun graduates featured strongly. Nine were MiG-21s and half the victories were attributed to two squadrons, VF-96 and VF-161 *Chargers*. Although the F-4J had already re-equipped most Phantom squadrons, ten kills were by F-4Bs, including several early production models that had long service records in USN and USMC units. Two of the VF-51 *Screaming Eagles* examples, BuNos 149473 and 149457, were delivered in 1962 and both survived the war. Both destroyed MiG-17s during the same *Linebacker* mission on June 11, 1972 when their crews intercepted four at 500ft altitude as the VPAF pilots were setting up an ambush near Than Hoa. Lts Winston "Mad Dog" Copeland and Don Bouchoux in BuNo 149457 *Eagle 113* were wingmen to Cdr Foster "Tooter" Teague and Lt Ralph Howell in *Eagle 114*. Neither of the veteran F-4Bs had serviceable radar and Copeland had no radio. Diving in behind the VPAF flight Copeland released an AIM-9G at the lead MiG pilot who had pulled up to try and gain a height advantage and attack *Eagle 114*, thereby putting himself in a perfect position for Copeland's missile, which exploded inside his tailpipe. Teague also fired from behind his adversary and the AIM-9G impacted inside the MiG and downed it. Copeland's aircraft took ground-fire hits near the coast and a fire started, melting one of the Sparrows into the airframe. He succeeded in recovering the wounded F-4B to USS *Coral Sea*, although it never flew operationally again.

E **F-4 MIG KILLERS**

Rootbeer flight from VF-33 *Tarsiers* on USS *America* was assigned a low-altitude combat air patrol mission (CAP) for a USN Alpha strike on July 10, 1968 at a time of fairly minimal MiG activity. Warning was given of two MiG-21s that were approaching A-7 Corsair IIs in the strike package. *Rootbeer* F-4Js accelerated to 550kts at low altitude and at four miles range. Lt Roy "Outlaw" Cash (nephew of singer Johnny Cash) and Lt Ed "Killer" Kain in *Rootbeer 212* (BuNo 155553) fired two AIM-7 missiles. The two MiGs turned at 90 degrees to the missiles, breaking the F-4J's Doppler radar tracking, but one VPAF pilot turned back towards Cash and he fired a Sidewinder outside its guidance parameters, which served to scare off the MiG wingman. *Rootbeer 212* was then steered behind the leading MiG-21 and Cash fired a second AIM-9G at 1,500ft range, blowing the tail section off the MiG. Its pilot ejected almost simultaneously. It was the first MiG kill for the F-4J model and for an Atlantic Coast F-4 unit. It was also the only aerial victory for a USN crew from USS *America*.

VF-51 and VF-92 each destroyed one of the eight MiGs that fell to USN Phantom squadrons on their most memorable day of aerial combat; 10 May 1972. The rest were added to VF-96's four victories and three of them made Lt Randall Cunningham and Lt(JG) Willy Driscoll into the Navy's only Vietnam aces. Lt Brian Grant, Cunningham's regular wingman, told the author that Cunningham was "a very instinctive fighter pilot and a very brave man who additionally worked harder at his craft and more often than any other pilot that I have ever known." F-4J BuNo 155800 had been launched on a flak suppression mission with a full load of Mk 20 Rockeye ordnance that day, dropped on a warehouse complex as no obvious flak sites were seen. Pulling off target they were approached by numerous MiG-17s and Cunningham downed one with an AIM-9 while Grant kept the MiG wingman occupied. Cunningham "dragged" another MiG-17 out in front of Grant to give him a shot but too many other enemy fighters started to pursue his Phantom. Cunningham then dived into a defensive "wagon wheel" of MiGs which included two F-4Js which were trying to get behind MiG-17s. Again, he called "Fox Two" (a Sidewinder launch) and his missile blew a second MiG apart. His final adversary was a better pilot and Cunningham defeated him by using the Top Gun-advocated tactic of fighting in the vertical plane. The MiG pilot followed him through three steep climbs but on the third ascent Cunningham throttled back, forcing the MiG to overshoot and dive ahead of the Phantom as both aircraft ran out of energy. Cunningham's third AIM-9 sent the MiG-17 into a terminal dive.

F-4s continued in fleet service postwar, although the first F-14A Tomcats had appeared in squadron service as the conflict ended. Their fleet defense mission in the Mediterranean, Atlantic, and Pacific required them to repel frequent probing flights by Soviet reconnaissance and bomber aircraft. Every Carrier Group Commander's nightmare was the prospect that photographs of an unescorted Soviet aircraft overflying his ships might be published. Tu-95 Bears and Tu-16 Badgers were therefore intercepted by Deck Alert F-4s at the limit of their range and turned away or escorted as they took their photographs or simulated antishipping missile attacks. Distracting techniques, such as powerful spotlights to disorientate pilots at night, were used by both sides but the exchanges were usually more cordial and included displays of *Playboy* centerfolds or vodka bottles.

USMC Phantoms

Marine F-4 VMFA (fighter-attack) squadrons were drawn into the Vietnam scenario soon after their six F-4B units had become operational. The first to deploy was VMFA-531 *Gray Ghosts* which deployed to Da Nang AB from Atsugi, Japan with eight KC-130F refuellers on May 10, 1965 within the 9th Marine Expeditionary Brigade. The base was still primitive with only limited supplies of World War II bombs at first. On their first napalm strike 11 of their 12 fire-bombs failed to ignite and the FAC (forward air controller), unfamiliar with the missiles-only F-4, suggested that the pilots should set off the napalm solution with gunfire. Crew members wore orange flight suits that were soon replaced by equally unsuitable heavy cloth camouflage outfits and eventually by standard flight garments. The squadron pioneered many of the tactics that occupied successive Marine F-4 units until the last squadrons left the area in September 1973. Many involved close air support (CAS) for Marines in contact with enemy ground forces and pilots quickly refined techniques for

firing up to six Aero 7D or LAU-10 pods of 2.75in. rockets or dropping napalm or Mk 82 bombs within very close proximity of "friendly" troops. Col Manfred Rietsch recalled, "During one mission when our 'grunts' were in deep trouble getting overrun I delivered 'nape' within 30 to 40ft of the friendlies, running parallel to their front line." Other demanding missions occurred at night against well-defended targets in mountainous terrain that were partially lit by parachute flares from AC-47s or C-130s.

Although the *Gray Ghosts* were well-practiced in air-to-air combat and had come close to intercepting MiG-17s during the Cuban Missile Crisis of 1963 there was little call for these skills in Vietnam. Marine airbases mounted a hot-pad air-to-air element of two F-4s in case of air attack, but they were never launched. Instead, the crews could be called upon to fly barrier combat patrol (BARCAP) missions offshore to protect the Task Force, often at night. These involved repetitive race-track patterns for up to 8 hours with occasional aerial refuelling to break the monotony and possibly a little unofficial ACM practice on the return leg. For many missions USMC F-4s carried no air-to-air missiles to save weight. However, they were appropriately armed for their frequent escort flights for nocturnal USMC A-6A interdiction missions, EF-10B and EA-6A electronic warfare aircraft, RF-4B recon flights and even *Arc Light* B-52 formations.

Some combat air patrols (CAP) were flown in the southern areas of North Vietnam, also RESCAP (rescue combat air patrol) missions for downed pilots and "LZ prep" sorties in which four F-4Bs would accompany a Marine helicopter force to a landing zone, clearing the way with pre-emptive rocket fire against likely ambush positions. The F-4B crews quickly developed a reputation for accuracy despite their rudimentary bombing avionics but on many occasions they had to fly TPQ-10 radar bombing missions when typically heavy cloud cover obscured their intended targets. From April 27, 1965 Marine Air Support Squadron 2 ran three teams to operate the helicopter-transportable TPQ-10 units that connected with Phantoms and other fighter-bombers via a narrow radar beam and transmitted a command signal to drop their bombs (typically, around 5,000lb) on pre-determined map coordinates. Cloud cover made target damage assessment difficult but commanders felt that the psychological effect of these unexpected "harassment and interdiction" attacks were worthwhile. During the monsoon season F-4

F-4S-28-MC BuNo 153792 in the very "lo-viz" 1981 markings of VMFA-312 *Checkerboards*, who flew Phantoms from February 1966 until their transition to F/A-18 Hornets in April 1988. The F-4J/S's J79-GE-10B engines were extremely reliable, with smooth afterburner operation, easy re-start and absence of surges or stalling. The width of its undercarriage track was a great advantage for deck landings. (US Navy)

F-4B-14-MC BuNo 150484, a former data-link F-4G, laden with CBU and Sargent Fletcher wing-tanks. USMC aircraft refueled from their own KC-130F tankers but the usual 200kts link-up speed was only around 20kts above an F-4B's stalling speed. This necessitated a high angle of attack and additional engine thrust for the F-4B, increasing fuel consumption by around 50 percent to 200lb per minute and burning off 20 percent of the transferred fuel during the refueling process. A heavy bomb-load complicated the process further, reducing the fighter's stability. (Mule Holmberg via Tailhook Association)

crews often flew two TPQ sorties each night for weeks. As they seldom ventured over North Vietnam, the risks of flying straight and level in formation were acceptable and over 38,000 of these missions were flown.

The increase in USMC firepower in Vietnam from mid-1965 took four more VMFA units and an RF-4B squadron to the area that year. For some it was the first of several deployments. VMFA-115 *Silver Eagles* was the longest-serving unit with six deployments from three bases, the last one ending in August 1973 after 34,000 combat sorties in all. The construction of a new coastal base at Chu Lai enabled two squadrons of F-4s and numerous A-4 Skyhawks to fly from a runway of AM-2 interlocking metal planks laid over sand and laterite soil with an aircraft-carrier catapult for launches and an M-21 MOREST cable arresting gear for recovery, complete with a mirror landing aid. Aircraft were refueled from 10,000 gallon bladder tanks. They could launch at 54,800lb with full fuel and 6,000lb of bombs. However, wear and tear on this facility required the building of a conventional 10,000ft concrete runway in 1966.

F-4 and RF-4B Phantoms from Marine Air Group 11 (MAG-11) and MAG-16 at Da Nang, with MAG-13 at Chu Lai were subjected to intensive use in their primary role of supporting USMC ground troops, but they increasingly supported US Army activity under 7th Air Force control as well, including air defense duties. VMFA-115 flew an unprecedented 717 combat sorties in July 1966, delivering almost 1,000 tons of ordnance. Other squadrons sustained similar levels of activity for months, often with fewer than ten serviceable aircraft each day from a total of about 20 per squadron. F-4 avionics did not take kindly to South East Asian climatic conditions and aircraft normally took around 40 maintenance man hours per flight hour to stay useable. Engine changes took 16 hours and a radio change took four. Early AN/AWG-10 radars often went down after a couple of flights and the F-4B's radar system tended to deteriorate rapidly. Disassembling, inspecting and reassembling an engine could take three to five men up to three weeks to complete.

In August 1966 each of VMFA-314's 16 assigned F-4Bs flew an average of 66 sorties. The Marine aviators' success in preventing US ground troops and installations from being overrun by overwhelming North Vietnamese forces was considerable. A typical VMFA-115 CAS sortie near Dong Ha by two F-4Bs with Mk 82s and gun-pods cost the enemy 195 fatalities. Crews were

often required to ignore the standard "one pass, haul ass" rule whereby ordnance was delivered and the aircraft withdrew before enemy gunners could respond. Repeated passes were often requested by FACs and ground commanders in desperate situations. A VMFA-314 *Black Knights* crew (1Lt Keenan and Capt C. Fairchild) made seven napalm passes against enemy trenches during Operation *Utah* before their F-4B (BuNo 151453) took lethal hits in its hydraulic systems.

Phantom squadrons played a crucial role in defending the USMC base at Khe Sanh. Many aircraft returned with severe damage or numerous small-arms hits that were patched up before yet another mission. Many of these were quick-reaction "hot pad" missions of short duration, sometimes to counter enemy forces within a few miles of the base. Being hit on take-off by a rifle bullet fired by an innocent-looking "farmer" working close to the airfield perimeter was a daily possibility. Aircraft were generally at their most vulnerable when pulling out from a bomb-run.

Although the end of *Rolling Thunder* brought some reduction in flight operations Marine F-4 units continued to pound targets in South Vietnam and Laos with squadrons such as VMFA-314 still averaging over 600 CAS and escort missions per month in 1969 and 1970. The extension of the conflict into Cambodia increased the load again: VMFA-314 flew 762 combat sorties in May 1970, hitting supply dumps, transport, and trench-lines. The general draw-down of US forces later in 1970 left VMFA-115 as the only USMC F-4 unit in theatre until March 1971. When the North Vietnamese invasion of the South began in March 1972 this squadron and VMFA-232 returned to Da Nang with MAG-15. They were immediately thrown into action against huge enemy forces with armor and concentrated troop formations. The introduction of SA-7 infra-red antiaircraft missiles was a new hazard but the squadron caused devastating losses to the enemy despite this. VMFA-212 joined the battle in April, hitting SAM sites from Da Nang. VMFA-115 moved to a new base at Nam Phong in Thailand with VMFA-232 *Red Devils* in June 1972.

Many of the missions from Nam Phong in the last stages of the war were BARCAPs and the *Red Devils* had their only MiG engagement on a mission

F-4J-35-MC BuNo 155801 of VMFA-232 *Red Devils* leaps off the runway with AIM-9B missiles aboard. This USMC unit operated from Chu Lai, Da Nang and Nam Phong airbases in South East Asia during the Vietnam War. The "red devil" logo worn during the Chu Lai deployment was later moved to the vertical tail. (USMC)

on August 26, 1972, when Motion Alpha section was vectored onto a MiG-21. Sadly, a series of tactical errors resulted in the loss of an F-4J to the MiG pilot's Atoll missile. However, VMFA-333 *Shamrocks*, the first USMC F-4 unit to deploy on a carrier, scored the Marines' only Vietnam MiG kill. Major Lee Lasseter and Capt John Cummings fired four Sparrows and two AIM-9s at an elusive MiG-21 during a CAP, but downed it with their penultimate AIM-9D.

Hawk Eyes

Throughout the war until July 1970 VMCJ-1 *Golden Hawks* provided the Marines with aerial reconnaissance and electronic warfare support, using 18 RF-4Bs (replacing RF-8As by December 1969), EF-10Bs (until October 1969) and EA-6As. Their use was just as intensive as the VMFAs' with at least six RF-4B missions on most days, each with two aircraft. Film imagery was most in demand by the Intelligence units but data from the aircraft's other sensors was also processed later in the war. On-site color processing was not available until June 1968. Missions were assigned as "photo" or "IR" (using the AN/AAS-18 infra-red set), with comparatively few using the AN/APQ-102 SLAR. The unit's first major task was to make a photo mosaic of the demilitarized zone (DMZ), which had been inadequately mapped previously. Five aircraft made a supersonic formation pass at 200ft to give the required coverage. RF-4Bs were needed for bomb damage assessment (BDA) and to identify enemy artillery positions near the DMZ. Crews relied on speed to survive, particularly when they knew they would be expected by enemy gunners shortly after a bombing attack. RF-4Bs often returned with small-arms damage but only four were lost.

Night-time IR missions were among the most hazardous as they were invariably flown at low altitudes. When the threat from southerly based MiGs increased in 1969 one RF-4B was unofficially field-rigged for self-defensive AIM-9 missiles. The squadron did receive Sanders AN/ALQ-81 external ECM pods and the Shoehorn Delta installation as protection against SAMs. In mid-1970 quick-reaction sorties were introduced for the 1st Marine Division. RF-4Bs over-flew up to ten targets on each flight and the film was "hot downloaded" with the aircraft's engines still running and processed within 30 minutes so that target information was still fresh enough for strike flights to catch the enemy.

Low visibility markings were also applied to the USMC's RF-4Bs in the 1980s. BuNo 157350 (seen in June 1988) was the penultimate RF-4B, complete with Block 6 Project SURE upgrades to its sensors, slotted stabilator, AN/ASN-92 carrier alignment INS, AN/ASW-25B data-link, new AN/APD-10B SLAR and AN/AAD-5 IR sets and the heavier F-4J undercarriage used for the last dozen aircraft. It also has the more rounded lower nose area of the final three RF-4Bs. (via K. Darling)

By the end of June 1970 VMCJ-1 had completed 25,000 missions and it withdrew to MCAS Iwakuni as part of the draw-down. In April 1972 a seagoing detachment (Det.101) was formed to operate from USS Midway with CVW-5. VMCJ-2 *Playboys* also took its RF-4Bs aboard USS *Forrestal* in 1971 and USS *Saratoga* in 1973 while VMCJ-3, the first RF-4B unit, continued to fly from MCAS El Toro until July 1975 when all three squadrons were amalgamated into VMFP-3 *Eyes of the Fleet*. An update program for the aircraft's sensors, INS and ECM equipment kept the surviving RF-4Bs current until their retirement in September 1990. Its absence during the Gulf War a few months later was sorely felt by USMC commanders.

Carrier-borne F-4N squadrons came close to action in the spring of 1980 when VMFA-531 and VMFA-323 deployed on USS *Coral Sea* for Operation *Eagle Claw*, the abortive rescue attempt for US hostages in Iran. Fourteen Marine units flew F-4J and F-4S Phantoms and several deployed on carriers to replace USN squadrons that were transitioning to the F-14A. The USMC selected the F/A-18 Hornet rather than the F-14A and its squadrons moved to the new McDonnell Douglas fighter from December 1982, leaving VMFA-112 *Cowboys* as the final USMC F-4 squadron in August 1992.

Royal Navy

The Royal Navy's only operational Phantom FG.1 squadron, 892 Sqn was commissioned on 31 March 1969 with 13 aircraft, commanded by Lt Cdr Brian Davies who had been closely involved in the testing and introduction of the aircraft. At that time 700P Sqn, the FG.1 Intensive Flying Trials Unit (IFTU) disbanded and training passed to 767 Sqn at RNAS Yeovilton from January 1969 with six ex-700P FG.1s commanded by Lt Cdr Peter Marshall. 767 Sqn also received five RAF FG.1s in 1969 for its ten instructors to train 43 Sqn RAF crews on the FG.1. The training program included "land-away" navigation exercises to European bases such as RAF Brüggen in West Germany, Leeuwarden in the Netherlands and Vaerlose in Denmark, and participation in Exercise *Capricorn*, a 1972 UK air defense exercise.

With Speys ablaze 892 Sqn's FG.1 XV567/003R blasts off from HMS *Ark Royal*'s deck in 1978. In November of that year it was repainted in RAF markings and reissued to 43 Sqn at Leuchars. The dark patches on the upper fuselage are antislip surfaces for ground crew safety. The FG.1's double-extension 40in. nose-wheel leg, essential for operations in hot, still-air tropical climates but deactivated in RAF service, was manually operated with a switch in the left undercarriage well. The increased AoA on take-off enabled a reduction of 11kts in the wind-over-deck speed needed for a carrier launch. Any deck-launched F-4 needed the control column to be pulled fully back for launch, swiftly followed by "forward stick" to prevent over-rotation and stalling. (Author's Collection)

Wing Commander Nick Spiller shuts down FGR.2 XT910/O on August 25, 1992 while Wattisham ground crew prepare to return the Phantom to its hardened aircraft shelter (HAS). This aircraft flew with five RAF squadrons from November 1968, including four periods with 228 OCU. A fully loaded FGR.2 weighed three times as much as the Hunter FGA.9 that it replaced. (Author)

Initial 892 Sqn carrier trials and operations were flown from HMS *Eagle* in June 1969 and USS *Saratoga*, with four aircraft attached to VF-103 *Sluggers* in October–November 1969 while HMS *Ark Royal* continued its extensive re-fit. Air defense sorties were flown with VF-103 during the political crises in Lebanon and Libya in 1970. The squadron also trained with 849B Sqn's early-warning Gannet AEW 3s and French Navy F-8E(FN) Crusaders. It had already gained public attention by participating in the *Daily Mail* Transatlantic Air Race on May 4–11, 1969 when three (in order to make sure that one was serviceable, as Lt Cdr Davies observed later) Project *Royal Blue* aircraft flew from Floyd Bennett NAS, New York to Wisley, Surrey with the best record time of 4hrs 46mins 57secs being attained by Lt Cdrs Davies and Peter Goddard in XT858. Their instant celebrity and the publicity for the "Rolls-Royce" Phantom was accompanied by the loan of a Rolls-Royce Silver Shadow car to be taken aboard *Ark Royal* for squadron use abroad. The squadron's primary purpose was fleet defense, with a secondary ground-attack role in support of ground forces during amphibious landings.

892 Sqn eventually embarked on *Ark Royal* on June 12, 1970, taking part in Exercise *Northern Wedding* in September although the Air Group disembarked again in October partly because the FG.1s were wearing out the arresting wire system. After repairs the carrier sailed to the Mediterranean led by Lt Cdr Kerr to begin eight years of operations with four major deployments supporting NATO commitments there, in the Caribbean and in the Atlantic as far as the Arctic Circle. Training with the USN continued, with a short embarkation on USS *Nimitz* in 1975 attached to VMFA-333 *Shamrocks* and several visits to US Navy F-4 shore bases. Cross-decking operations were

conducted with USS *Independence* and USS *Enterprise* in 1975, including aerial refueling from A-7 Corsair "buddy-tankers." *Ark Royal* and the USS *John F. Kennedy* waged a mock "carrier war" against each other off Florida in 1976. Weapons training with both missiles and bombs took place in Sardinia and over the Atlantic. The run-down of the carrier force hit RN aircrew recruitment; by the end of the last *Ark Royal* embarkation half the FG.1 (and Buccaneer) aircrews were RAF personnel.

RAF supervision of naval fixed-wing flying support took 892 Sqn from RNAS Yeovilton to RAF Leuchars in September 1972 and FG.1 training with 767 Sqn at Yeovilton then ended, replaced by the Phantom Training Flight (PTF) at Leuchars. The PTF produced crews for 43 Sqn's FG.1s and for 111 Sqn which moved to Leuchars in November 1975 ready to take over 892 Sqn's FG.1s when it disbanded on December 1, 1978 after a final farewell Mediterranean cruise. All training passed to 228 OCU in May 1978.

RAF

The RAF Phantom FGR.2's service history occurred in two phases. The first, from 1969 to the mid-1970s was focused on RAF Coningsby, home of the FGR.2 Fighter-Bomber/Strike/Attack force (FBSA), and RAF Brüggen, West Germany, base for the RAF Germany FBSA, with another FGR.2 unit for reconnaissance. From 1975 the strike/attack and army cooperation role passed to SEPECAT Jaguar GR.1s and the versatile Phantoms took over air defense duties in the UK and West Germany. At Coningsby 228 OCU, the longest-serving UK Phantom unit was established on August 1, 1968. It had trained 1,320 crews by the time of its disbandment on January 31, 1991. Its first 13 crews went to 6 Sqn, the first operational squadron, which worked within No. 38 Group from May 6, 1969 under Wg Cdr Harcourt-Smith. Its "B" Flight commander, Sqn Ldr Anthony "Bugs" Bendell described the Phantom as "the first multi-role aircraft in RAF service since the remarkable Mosquito" and a major advance on the Hawker Hunter for ground attack. However, its radar ranging had to be backed up by skill and experience for accurate bombing.

19 Sqn FGR.2 XT899 flew the last QRA mission at Wildenrath with similarly painted XV408/Z on 92 Sqn on March 31, 1992. XT899's markings commemorated 19 Sqn's 76 years of service on its disbandment in 1991. Wing Commander Nick Spiller described the blue jet as "a pig to fly – not nearly as nice as the other aircraft in our fleet, but it did look exceptionally smart in its blue color scheme." After brief additional service at Wattisham it was flown to the Prague-Kbely Museum in the Czech Republic, "the first British fighter to cross the Iron Curtain intentionally since World War II," as Spiller pointed out. He had arranged for the names of Flt Lt Phil Williamson and Sqn Ldr John Teague, 19 Sqn's most experienced members, to be painted on the canopy for the delivery flight. Wildenrath's maintainers replaced these names with the names of the delivery crew (Geoff Bridle and Al Palfrey), neither of whom had flown with 19 Sqn. (Author)

Ordnance practice, mainly at low altitudes, and close support sorties were combined with reconnaissance flights carrying a strike camera in the left front missile well. Later, 6 Sqn trained with the Lepus parachute flare, dropped from the leading Phantom to provide five minutes of target illumination for night reconnaissance, or bombing by aircraft following the "flare ship." On UK ranges such as Tain or Otterburn delivery of retarded bombs, SNEB rockets and gun-pod strafing was practiced. The gun-pod proved to be particularly devastating against vehicular targets. Visits to RAF Wildenrath and the first armament practice camp at RAF Akrotiri, Cyprus, followed in the fall including a simulated attack on the base and its Lightning defenders. Participation in NATO's *Arctic Express* exercise in February 1970 took 6 Sqn to snowy Norway.

The squadron was joined on September 1, 1969 by 54 Sqn. On July 12, 1972 41 Sqn formed, specializing in tactical reconnaissance with the EMI reconnaissance pod. No. 2 Sqn in West Germany laid the groundwork for use of the pods. In May 1970 two 54 Sqn FGR.2s led by Sqn Ldr John Nevill set a new record for the 8,680-mile flight to Tengah, Singapore, completed non-stop in 14hrs 6mins 55.6secs. This became a regular annual deployment for 6 and 54 Sqns. Various tactics were developed for nuclear and conventional strikes, a favorite being the escort formation in which a strike element was followed by another pair about a mile behind it to trap any hostile interceptors. In daylight crews tended to navigate visually rather than by radar and INAS, flying at around 420kts and 250ft. Crews soon developed confidence in the Phantom and its systems, realizing its superiority to other contemporary strike aircraft as they worked with an increasingly wide selection of other NATO units.

The introduction of the Jaguar GR.1 from June 1974 into Nos. 6 and 54 Sqns curtailed their Phantom-flying period although some crews and aircraft were reassigned to 111 Sqn at Leuchars which formed in November 1975 and absorbed ex-Royal Navy FG.1s from March 1978, converting to the Tornado F.3 in 1990. Its re-equipment with Phantoms initiated the gradual phase-out of the Lightning. Assigned to 11 Group in RAF Strike Command 43 Sqn, the only RAF Phantom interceptor unit from 1969 to 1975, was also based at Leuchars with its air defense and maritime protection FG.1s, known locally as the "North Sea Sports GT Models." It began Quick Reaction Alert (QRA) operations in March 1970 and continued to fly Phantoms until July 1979. Many regarded transition to the Jaguar as a retrograde step, although its small size, good low-altitude performance and advanced nav-attack system possibly compensated for its less muscular image.

2ATAF Striker

Having established a UK-based Phantom strike force, 228 OCU began to train pilots to man RAF Germany squadrons alongside the newly equipped 2nd Allied Tactical Air Forces (2ATAF) Harrier GR.3 and Buccaneer S.2 units guarding the northern sector of the NATO Central Region. Three ex-Canberra squadrons were prepared: 14, 17, and 31 Sqns in 1970–71, with 2 Sqn converting from Hunter FR.10s in December 1970 at Brüggen and moving to Laarbruch, West Germany in April 1971 with aircraft modified for the EMI pod. Brüggen strike aircraft were on call for interdiction, ground attack, nuclear strike and CAS within a 240-mile radius where they would have faced heavy, layered defenses and numerically superior air forces. Nuclear strikes would have been flown by single aircraft against pre-planned targets, delivering the "special" weapon at low altitude. Aircraft stood on QRA in an isolated top-security "shed" with live nuclear weapons at all times, ready to respond to a sudden mass advance by Soviet forces. Many pilots scheduled to attack specific Warsaw Pact targets estimated their chances of returning at less than 50 percent.

Wing Cdr Nick Spiller described the RAFG (RAF Germany) FGR.2 as "a battering ram fighter in the traditional sense rather than an interceptor. The great thing about it was its hitting power. It was a heavyweight fighter with eight missiles. Germany was a very exciting theatre because we were operating with so many different nations; a great challenge." The purpose of the Mixed Fighter Force concept, devised by the RAF and USAF at Soesterberg air base, Netherlands, was to, "take the German F-4F Phantoms, which didn't have a decent Doppler radar at the time, and the F-104s into the fight. The F-15 Eagle was the kingpin and the FGR.2 was the second among NATO fighters as it had Doppler radar and long-range BVR missiles." Counter air missions were aimed at airfields, with free-fall bombs delivered by toss or dive bombing. Interdiction missions were to hit logistical choke-points, troop concentrations and communications. For close support, crews were tasked with support of army units near the battle front, managed by a forward air controller. Low-altitude flying was central to all missions and some missiles were carried for self defense. RAFG strike crews spent little time on in-flight refueling practice and the FGR 2s' redundant refueling probes were temporarily deactivated in the early 1970s.

Air Defender

After roughly five years as a primary striker the FGR.2 was released to Air Defence squadrons, replacing Lightnings. Pilots initially found the Phantom's performance less spectacular than the Lightning's but its vastly superior weaponry, radar, two-man crew and range made it far better suited to the task. Within the 4 million square miles of the UK Air Defence Region (UKADR) the Phantom's role resembled that of its USN F-4B/J forebears – the long-distance interception of bombers armed with stand-off missiles at all altitudes and in all weather conditions. The opposition in 1975 consisted of Tu-22M Backfires, Su-24 Fencers and Tu-95 Bear reconnaissance/bombers. The Phantom force was reorganized at three bases to cover the UK. For the Northern section 43 and 111 Sqns remained at Leuchars, 29 and 64 (a frontline squadron within 228 OCU) operated from Coningsby as the Center region, and former Lightning operators 29 and 56 Sqns were based at RAF Wattisham for the "Southern Q" Sector. Two Lightning F.3/F.6 units remained at Binbrook until 1987. All were supported by tankers, "Anyface"-coded Shackleton Mk.2 AEW aircraft, Bloodhound and Rapier missiles. QRA duties were rotated between the bases with 24-hour alerts manned for two aircraft at ten minutes readiness, "cocked and ready to go," for about a month. A second pair of aircraft immediately replaced them when they scrambled and a third set of crews could be summoned within minutes.

At Wattisham the Southern QRA required two crews to remain on duty for 24 hours from 8am. This, as Flt Lt Mark Manwaring explained, was followed by a "Q stand-down" the next day for them.

When a squadron was holding QRA there were 8 aircrew on "Q" or "Q stand-down"; quite a lot of the squadron, plus two aeroplanes and six engineers working seven days on, seven days off. When we lost the QRA at Wattisham we realised what a drain on manpower it had been. We scrambled during Soviet exercises over the North Sea. On one we had six FGR.2s airborne and we were calling up the "Q 7" crew. I was "Q 2" that night. We intercepted two Bears and had to divert to Keflavik. It was so busy that the tanker ran out of gas and we were nearer to Iceland than Scotland.

When Soviet trespassers became numerous all three bases would launch QRA flights. Each bomber had to be identified by reading the number painted on its nose-wheel door and small structural modifications were noted and photographed. At night this often meant close proximity to a massive Bear and exposure to the teeth-loosening roar of its 14,800hp NK-12 engines or the dazzling glare of a searchlight, aimed at the Phantom crew. In one week of April 1980 111 Sqn was scrambled for over 100 interceptions of Soviet "traffic," although 4–5 scrambles per week was more usual. Interception tactics were regularly practiced in exercises like *Elder Forest* involving up to 200 NATO aircraft, or *Mallet Blow*. With the phase-out of the RN aircraft carriers Leuchars was also tasked with maritime defense, requiring missions of up to 7 hours to protect naval forces. Defensive Combat Air Patrols, with two Phantoms flying "race-track" patterns at around 15,000ft, were also flown at three locations offshore in emergencies.

No. 29 Sqn at Coningsby replaced 6 Sqn and also 29 Sqn (AD) at Wattisham which continued to fly Lightnings until the end of December 1974. At Leuchars 23 (AD-Lightning) Sqn became 23 (AD-Phantom) Sqn, transferring to Coningsby on November 1, 1975 and thence to Wattisham where it became operational on May 14, 1976. It remained there until March 30, 1983 when it was re-formed in the Falklands as 29 Sqn, taking over the defense of the islands from the three-aircraft RAF 29(F) Detachment that had mounted QRA from Ascension Island since May 25, 1982. This was followed postwar by a nine-aircraft presence at Port Stanley, commanded by 29 Sqn CO, Wg Cdr Ian Macfadyen, from October 17. For a year the crews lived on a converted ferry boat in Stanley Harbour and flew from a 4,000ft runway, extended for Phantom operations by a steel plank section with five arresting wires. They usually flew with eight missiles, a gun-pod and wing-tanks. Their presence deterred any additional Argentinian incursions, but there is little doubt that the invasion of the Falklands could have been prevented altogether if HMS *Ark Royal*'s Phantoms and Buccaneers had still been available in 1982.

F

PHANTOMS OVER GERMANY

Phantom IIs equipped seven RAF strike-reconnaissance squadrons from 1969 until they were replaced by Jaguar GR.1s from August 1974 onwards. Second Allied Tactical Air Force (2ATAF) Phantom FGR.2s, like this 17 Sqn aircraft (XT 905) from RAF Brüggen, specialized in interdiction, close air support and strike missions. Many of these were flown at very low altitudes at 360–420kts in poor weather conditions using INAS and traditional time-and-distance navigation. For wartime close support missions, crews would have found potential targets for their SUU-23/A gun-pods (useful also for air-to-air defense) or SNB 68mm rockets. AIM-7 missiles were not usually carried on training missions. XT 905 was one of the RAF's dual-control FGR.2s with flight controls in the rear cockpit and it served with 228 OCU, the Phantom training unit, as well as four other squadrons. No. 17 was the second RAF Germany squadron to operate the Phantom and in 2003 it became the first RAF squadron to fly the Eurofighter Typhoon. Ten years later, as 17 Test and Evaluation Squadron, it was responsible for the introduction of the F-35B Lightning II to RAF service.

At the end of 1983 these aircraft were taken over by 23 Sqn and then, with only four aircraft at the new Mount Pleasant airbase it was renamed once again as No. 1435 Flight in November 1988. To complete the Phantom restructuring 56 Sqn replaced 23 Sqn at Coningsby from 31 March 1976, moving to Wattisham to replace 56 (AD-Lightning) on June 29, 1976 and remaining there until disbandment on June 30, 1992. Wattisham was also home to the last RAF Phantom squadron to form. No. 74 Tiger Sqn re-formed in July 1984 to fill gaps in the UKADR caused by the deployment of FGR.2s to the Falklands. Flying the F-4J(UK), it was commissioned on October 19 and converted to FGR.2s as they became available in January 1991, ceasing F-4 operations on 30 September 1992.

Defending Germany

From January 1977 the two RAFG Lightning interceptor squadrons, 19 and 92 Sqns, also converted from Lightnings to the FGR.2, manning QRAs until 1991. Although the potential enemy substantially outnumbered the Phantom force, Soviet-trained pilots were considered too reliant on rigid ground-control guidance. They lacked air superiority training and their weapons systems were judged to be inferior to the Phantom's. With a 70-mile radar range for bomber-sized targets (40–50 for fighters, reducing to about 20 miles at low altitude) the F-4 navigator could use multi-bar scans to detect multiple targets at long range, narrowing the radar search on their relatively small radar screens to a single-bar scan to attack a selected target. There were manual back-up methods for the radar and Sparrows that could defeat ECM interference with their automatic functions, giving the F-4 a good chance against any aerial opponent.

UK QRA reaction time was defined partly by the time required to warm up and align the INAS, although crews usually met their "Readiness 10" (minutes) targets. A less accurate 90-second quick alignment was possible if the INAS oil was warmed from an external source. At RAF Wildenrath, West Germany the reaction time was reduced to a strict five minutes to take-off, the best time achieved by any NATO base. Nick Spiller explained:

> QRA was the major driver of your life. The first concern was always, "Are we meeting our Battle Flight commitment?" The whole station was geared to this. Wildenrath took over the QRA commitment on 1 January 1977 and didn't drop it until 20 October 1991. This is a long time to have aircraft and crews in a high state of readiness and it required a lot of effort.

In Wing Cdr Spiller's case that commitment lasted for 22 years, 15 of them in RAF Germany, after he joined 19 Sqn in November 1969. As an extra responsibility, six Wildenrath FGR.2s were detached to Akrotiri on August 17, 1990, replacing Tornado F.3s in the defense of Cyprus as part of Operation *Granby*.

The pressures of maintaining QRA had their lighter side. Nick Spiller:

> Wing Cdr Anthony "Bugsy" Bendell was the first commander of 19 Sqn on FGR.2s and he was very concerned about a forthcoming TACEVAL [NATO Tactical Evaluation], which dominated our lives in those days. He was worried that we wouldn't be able to scramble two Phantoms inside 5 minutes. One Saturday he was on QRA when the hooter went off. It was a fake alarm, but as he climbed into the cockpit he smashed his mic/tel lead that gave him all his information via the radio. When he was strapped in he could not talk to anyone. Not wanting to let the side down on a TACEVAL he started

the engines. His navigator, wondering what the hell was going on, tried gesticulating to stop him but nothing was going to prevent the wing commander from getting airborne inside his 5 minutes. He lined up on the runway and the navigator thought, "If I leave my canopy open he won't take off." Then he heard the burners light and the aircraft was last seen rushing down the runway with the navigator swinging on the canopy trying to get it closed before they took off. They did get airborne but didn't know where to go so they spent an hour orbiting over Wildenrath, burning the fuel down to landing weight. This caused its own merriment as one of the biggest gliding championships of all time was taking place and its route took it virtually over the top of Wildenrath, so the navigator was constantly ducking as gliders whizzed past on either side.

Battle Flight/QRA routines normally were honed to a fine art. Inside the stark green hardened aircraft shelter (HAS) the navigator checked the cockpit safety switches while the pilot did the "walk-around" inspection. Booster pumps and the radio were switched on and engines were started. With check-lists completed the aircraft took off in a pair, or in a stream with 30 seconds' separation. Practice interceptions, often at 250–500ft altitude, involved initial engagement with radar at long range, with visual identification, day or night, closer in. Ideally, a head-on Sparrow launch would precede a stern Sidewinder follow-up in the classic attack/re-attack (ARA) tactic. Although gun-pod practice was an annual event, the Phantom was "a stand-off fighter" as Nick Spiller explained. "If we did get into a turning, burning fight – a "doggers" – we had blown it, except that we still had the gun to get us out of trouble if we did have to engage at close quarters. It was a burden to carry around and a big fuel burner."

The alert status was maintained with relatively few aircraft. RAFG units each declared ten Phantoms (later increased to 11) to NATO and about seven would usually be available with two as reserves. Ideally, squadron leaders would have liked 18 aircraft, like the Dutch and Belgian NATO units.

CONCLUSION

Lt Gen Tom Miller, the first holder of an F-4 World Speed Record and the USMC officer most responsible for the US Marines' Phantom acquisition, summed up the F-4 Phantom II for this author:

> The McDonnell F-4 will certainly be recorded in aviation history as one of the greatest military aircraft ever produced. There are several factors that support this forecast. First, and probably the most amazing, was that it took only six years from the first contract until the first aircraft was delivered to the fleet in June 1961. Also, the F-4 set more World Performance Records (15) than any other military aircraft and it was used as a tactical fighter-bomber by more domestic and foreign air forces than any other aircraft in the world.

Lt Gen Miller compared the F-4's six-year development with the 20 years required for the V-22 Osprey procurement process under a far more complex decision-making process. He would probably have been unsurprised by similar delays between the 1996 development contract for the Marines' F-35B Lightning II and its projected Initial Operational Capability date of December 2016, or by the F-35B's projected $208m unit cost within the world's largest and most expensive aircraft program.

VX-4's F-4J BuNo 153088 "Screaming Eagle," with an F-4B radome and maneuvering slats, wore this spectacular Bicentennial scheme in 1976. It was retired to the Naval Air Technical Training Center Millington, in Memphis, Tennessee in August 1985. (US Navy)

The F-4 was clearly a far less sophisticated aircraft than the F-35 but its designers nevertheless had to resolve major technical challenges in producing a fighter that is still a credible warplane, still in service almost 60 years after its first flight and the world's best fighter for at least 15 of those years. Their ingenuity in designing the first multi-role jet combat aircraft to enter service required considerable innovation. Radically changing requirements from its potential customers and shifts in the political climate demanded frequent re-shaping of the original design. Throughout its gestation James S. McDonnell, "Mr Mac," was confident that it would become his company's biggest success and of greater long-term importance than his contracts for the Mercury and Gemini spacecraft that initiated American participation in the space race.

USN and USMC Phantom crews refined and expanded the F-4's intended role as fleet defense interceptor. They scored their share of the F-4's 280 MiG kills and forged aerial combat tactics for the aircraft that were adopted by many other users. In their hands the aircraft became an effective ground attack, reconnaissance and interdiction weapon in the skies of Vietnam, while still keeping Soviet intruders at a safe distance from the US fleet worldwide.

For the RAF the Phantom replaced a point-defense bomber interceptor, the BAC Lightning, with a multi-role aircraft with much better armament and twice the fuel capacity. Its radar was a huge improvement on those in its all-weather predecessors, the Sea Vixen and Gloster Javelin, and in its ground-attack role it represented a quantum leap in capability over the Hunter FGA.9 and Canberra B(I)8. Although the use of Spey engines, regarded as a political necessity, degraded the F-4K/M's performance, in some respects the reduced smoke emissions and good low-altitude fuel economy were advantages in its roles as fleet defender and long-range strike-reconnaissance vehicle. For the Royal Navy the partnership of 12 FG.1s and 14 Buccaneer S.2s made HMS *Ark Royal* a formidable weapon at the center of the British fleet for eight years.

During its long service career Phantom crews grew accustomed to its vicissitudes, including the "stall-spin" tendency which caused many accidents earlier on. Mark Manwaring: "The FGR.2 was not prone to stall-spin if handled within AoA limits. An arbitrary figure for optimum turn was 19 units of AoA but it could be flown up to 25 units as long as you didn't use aileron, just the rudder to get roll. Using aileron would make it flick and spin."

Towards the end of their RAF careers Phantom FGR.2s were equipped with a digital computer sighting system (DCSS) radar update, chaff and flare systems and a new HOTAS control column top. As Wing Cdr Nick Spiller explained, the latter was similar to the F/A-18 in placing all weapon controls in one place. "The front-seater could select, fire or jettison all ordnance without letting go of the throttle. Together with Skyflash and the AIM-9L this put the F-4 back in the game with the F-15 and F-16, making it a fighter that could have gone on for another ten years."

Further upgrades such as AMRAAM AIM-120 missiles or APG-65 radar were ruled out in favor of funding for the Tornado F.3 and Eurofighter Typhoon. While the RN Phantoms were the victims of a major alteration in UK government policy the RAF Phantom fleet was sacrificed to comply with the limitations of the Conventional Armed Forces in Europe Treaty, although maintenance costs for the aging airframes were also a factor. In 1992 most FGR.2 airframes averaged 5,000 hours and one had clocked up 5,700 hours – a good return on an airframe that was originally conceived for 1,000 hours. Reinforcements had added 1,800lb to the net weight and a re-sparring program in the late 1980s added another 400lb but doubled the fatigue life, enabling the fighter to operate beyond the year 2000. As Flt Lt Mark Manwaring ruefully pointed out to this author, "It was poignant that the day we did our final fly-past of the F-4J [with 74 Sqn in January 1991] was Day One of the Gulf War."

74 Sqn FGR.2 XV474/T about to lift off from RAF Wattisham's runway in August 1992 in the final months of RAF Phantom operations. This aircraft, fitted with a TESS sight, is preserved in the Imperial War Museum's Duxford collection. TESS, a telescopic sighting system, was installed on a metal canopy panel in some FGR.2s. It used an army tank-type optical sight for the navigator to identify aerial targets at 4–7 miles, allowing head-on Sparrow attacks. It was not fitted to "2-stick" (dual control) Phantoms as it further reduced the navigator's already poor visibility. (Author)

FURTHER READING

Books

Bendell, Anthony, *Never in Anger* (Orion, 1998)

Black, Ian, *The Last of the Phantoms* (Patrick Stephens, 2002)

Burns, Michael, *McDonnell Douglas F-4K and F-4M Phantom II* (Osprey Publishing, 1984)

Chesneau, Roger, *McDonnell Phantom FG MK 1/ FGR Mk 2* (Aeroguide 13, Linewrights, 1986)

Coremans, Danny, *Uncovering the US Navy F-4 Phantom* (Daco Publications, 2009)

Cunningham, Randy and Ethell, Jeff, *Fox Two* (Champlin Fighter Museum, 1984)

Davies, Peter E., *Gray Ghosts – US Navy and Marine Corps F-4 Phantoms* (Schiffer Publishing, 2000)

Davies, Peter E., *US Marine Corps F-4 Phantom II Units of the Vietnam War* (Osprey Publishing, 2012)

Davies, Peter, *USN F-4 Phantom II vs VPAF MiG-17/19* (Osprey Publishing, 2009)

Dorr, Robert F., *McDonnell Douglas F-4 Phantom II* (Osprey Publishing, 1984)

Elward, Brad and Davies, Peter, *US Navy F-4 Phantom II MiG Killers, 1965–70* (Osprey Publishing, 2001)

Elward, Brad and Davies, Peter, *US Navy F-4 Phantom II MiG Killers 1972–73,* (Osprey Publishing, 2002)

Ethell, Jeffrey and Price, Alfred, *One Day in a Long War* (Greenhill Books, 1989)

Foster, Gary Wayne, *Phantom in the River* (Hellgate Press, 2010)

Francillon, René J., *Tonkin Gulf Yacht Club* (Conway Maritime Press, 1988)

Giehl, Franz-Josef, *The F-4 Phantom II and the US Sixth Fleet in the Mediterranean* (Vantage Press, 1976)

Gunston, Bill, *F-4 Phantom* (Modern Combat Aircraft 1, Ian Allan, 1977)

Harty, John J., *The Business History of the F-4 Program* (McDonnell Aircraft Company, c. 1990)

Harty, John J., *F-4 Phantom II Program Milestones* (McDonnell Aircraft Company, 1988)

Kinzey, Bert, *F-4 Phantom II, USN and USMC Versions: In Detail and Scale* (Aero Publishers, 1983)

Martin, Patrick and Klein, Andreas, *US Navy Phantoms 1960–2004* (Double Ugly! Books, 2010)

Mersky, Peter B. and Polmar, Norman, *The Naval Air War in Vietnam* (The Nautical and Aviation Publishing Company of America, 1981)

Miller, Jay, *McDonnell RF-4 Variants* Aerofax Minigraph 13 (Aerofax, 1984)

Moulds, Sqn Ldr Gordon, *The Phantom OCU 1968–1991* (Holmes McDougall, 1992)

Nichols, Cdr John B. and Tillman, Barrett, *On Yankee Station* (Naval Institute Press, 1987)

O'Connor, Michael, *MiG Killers of Yankee Station* (New Past Press, 2003)

Peake, William R., *F-4 Phantom II Production and Operational Data* (Midland Publishing, 2004)

Prest, Robert, *F-4 Phantom, A Pilot's Story* (Cassell, 1979)

Stoffey, Col Robert E. and Holloway, Adm. James L., *Fighting to Leave* (Zenith Press, 2008)

Thornborough, Anthony and Davies, Peter E., *The Phantom Story* (Cassell, 2000)

Tillman, Barrett with van der Lugt, Henk, *VF-11/111 Sundowners* (Osprey Publishing, 2010)

Trotti, John, *Phantom over Vietnam* (Airlife, 1985)

Ward, Richard L., *Phantom Squadrons of the Royal Air Force and Fleet Air Arm* (Linewrights, 1988)

Wilcox, Robert K., *Scream of Eagles* (John Wiley & Sons, 1990)

Documents

NAVAIR 01-245FDB-1 *NATOPS Flight Manual F-4B Aircraft* (Department of the Navy, 1968)

NAVAIR 01-245FDD-1 *NATOPS Flight Manual F-4J Aircraft* (Department of the Navy, 1975)

NAVWEPS 01-245FDC-1 *NATOPS Flight Manual RF-4B Aircraft* (Department of the Navy, 1965)

McDonnell Aircraft Company, *F-4 Program History* (1992)

McDonnell Aircraft Company, *Plane Captain's Handbook, F-4B, F-4J, RF-4B* (1967)

McDonnell Aircraft Company, *RF-4B Multiple Sensor Reconnaissance Aircraft* (1963)

INDEX

Page numbers in **bold** refer to illustrations and their captions.

ailerons 12, 19, 20, 29, 61
air combat maneuvering (ACM) 40, **43**, 47
airframes **6**, 7, 8, 11, 14, **15**, 18, 26, 35, 44, 61
angle of attack (AoA) 14, 19, 28, 35, **51**, 61
antennas 8, **12**, **16**, 17, 27, 32, 34
anti-aircraft artillery (AAA) 40, **43**
   AAA-4 8, 27, 29
Atlantic, the **E44**, 46, 52, 53
   Fleet **9**, 26, 36, 40

barrier combat air patrol (BARCAP) 40, 42, 47, 49
bombs 10, 16, 22, 23, **B24**, **36**, 40, 41, 46, 47, **48**, 49, 50, 53, 54, 55
   BLU-27 fire-bombs 23, **B24**, 46; bombers 4, 5, 6, 8, 10, 12, 14, 46, 47, 53, 55, 56, 58, 59, 60; bombing 7, 9, 22, 26, 27, 39, 40, **41**, 47, 50, 53, 54, 55; cluster bomb unit (CBU) 23, 41, **48**; Mk 81 22, 23, **B24**; Mk 82 22, 23, **B24**, 27, **29**, **40**, **42**, 47, 48; SUU-23/A (XM-25) **B24**, **26**, **F56**
boundary layer control (BLC) 16, 19, 35
Britain 6, 14, **15**, **16**, **21**, **B24**, 26, 29, 30, 31, **32**, **35**, 51, **53**, 54, 55, 58, 60, 61

California 10, 30, 34, **35**, **43**
close air support (CAS) 27, 46, 48, 49, 54

Da Nang 11, **A12**, 46, 48, **49**
defensive electronic countermeasures (DECM) 29, 30, 34, **D36**

electronic countermeasures (ECM) 6, 12, 28, 29, **40**, 50, 51, 58
engines 5, 6, 7, 9, 10, 14, **15**, 16, 17, 18, **20**, **21**, 28, 30, 32, 42, 48, 50, 56, 59
   General Electric (GE): J79 **6**, 7, 9, 10, 14, 15, 19, 20, 21, 26, 27, 29, 30, 34, 35, **47**; Spey 14, **15**, **16**, 17, **21**, 26, 31, **51**, 60; thrust 16, 43, **48**; turbofans 16, **21**, 30; twin 5, 7, 9, 18

fin caps **16**, 27, 32, **39**, **40**
flaps 12, **17**, 19, 20
fuselage 7, 8, 15, 16, 17, 18, 27, 30, 34
   lower 8, 31; rear **16**, 18, 29, 31, 32; upper 20, 41, **51**

Germany 14, 55, **F56**, 58
   West **C32**, 51, 53, 54, 58
gun-pods 23, **B24**, **26**, 48, 54, **F56**, 59

hardened aircraft shelter (HAS) 34, **52**, 59
HMS *Ark Royal* 31, **C32**, 52, 53, 60

inertial navigation system (INS) 30, **41**, **50**, 51
infra-red imaging 8, 11, 22, 26, 28, 49, 50
   AN/AAS-18 infra-red imaging set 11, 28, 50
integrated navigation-attack system (INAS) 15, 32, 34, 54, **F56**, 58
   Ferranti 15, 32, 34

jet fighters 4, **5**, **6**, 7, 8, 9, 12, 14, **17**, 18, **19**,

27, 28, 31, 32, 38, 40, 43, 46, 47, **48**, 51, **53**, 55, 58, 59, 60, 61
Grumman F-14A Tomcat **9**, 12, 29, 46, 51; MiG 9, **A12**, 21, **23**, **34**, **39**, 40, 41, 42, 43, **E44**, 46, 49, 50, 60; MiG-17 **39**, **40**, 43, 46; MiG-21 **43**, **E44**, 50; VMFA-333 *Shamrocks* **29**, 50, 52

landing gear 12, 16, **17**, 18, 20
launcher unit (LAU): LAU-3/A **B24**, 40; LAU-10 23, **B24**, 47

Mach: 1.2 10; 1.4 23; 1.6 10; 1.9 31; 1.94 16; 2 8, 9; 2.1 16; 2.2 10; 2.41 9; 3.5 22
Manwaring, Flt Lt Mark "Manners" 30, 55, 61
McDonnell Douglas F-4 Phantoms 4, 31, 36, 51
   F3H Demon 4, **5**, 39; F-4 4, 10, **12**, 14, 15, **17**, 21, 26, 27, 30, 31, 35, **D36**, 38, **39**, 40, 41, 42, 43, **E44**, 46, 47, 48, 49, 50, **51**, 52, 58, 59, 60, 61; F4D Skyray 5, 8, **9**, 36; F/A-18 Hornets 27, **D36**, **47**, 51, 61; F-4A (F4H-1F) **9**, 26, 27, 28; F-4B (F4H-1) 9, 10, 11, **A12**, 14, 16, **18**, 19, 22, 23, **27**, **28**, 29, 31, **34**, 35, **36**, 38, **39**, **40**, 41, 42, 43, 44, 46, 47, **48**, 49, 55, **60**; F-4G **28**, 29; F-4J **11**, **A12**, 14, 15, **16**, **17**, **18**, **20**, 21, 22, **23**, 28, **29**, 30, 31, **A32**, 34, **35**, **D36**, 39, **42**, **43**, **E44**, 46, **47**, 49, **50**, 51, 58, **60**, 61; F-4K (Phantom FG.1) **15**, 16, 17, 31, 32, 35; F-4K/M 16, 21, 23, 35, 60; F-4M (FGR.2) 15, 26, 31, 32, 34, 35; F-4N 14, **28**, 29, 31, **34**, 35, **39**, 51; F-4S **9**, 12, 20, **21**, 22, 23, 30, 34, **35**, **D36**, **44**, **47**, 51; QF-4B 27, 34, 36; RF-4B **4**, 10, **11**, 12, 17, 27–8, 35, 47, 48, **50**, 51
missiles 5, 6, 7, 8, 14, 20, **21**, 22, **23**, 27, 29, 38, 39, 40, 42, 43, **E44**, 46, 47, 49, 50, 53, 54, 55, 56, 61
   air intercept missiles (AIM): Sidewinders 6, 8, 10, 11, 22, **23**, **B24**, 29, **34**, **42**, **43**, **E44**, 46, 59; AIM-9 11, 39, 46, 50; AIM-9B 8, 22, **49**; AIM-9D 1C 22, 23, 42, 50; AIM-9G 22, **23**, **B24**, **29**, **40**, **42**, **43**, **E44**; AIM-9H 22; AIM-9L 22, 24, 61; AIM-9M 22; Sidewinder expanded acquisition mode (SEAM) 22, 34; Sparrow 5, 6, 8, 10, 11, 21, 22, **23**, **B24**, 26, 38, 40, 44, 50, 58, 59, **61**; AIM-7 8, 10, 39, 40, **E44**, **F56**; AIM-7C 5, 21, 22, 36; AIM-7D 22; AIM-7E 22, **23**, **B24**, 42, **43**; BAe Skyflash 24, 30, 61; combat air patrol (CAP) **23**, 27, **E44**, 47, 50

napalm 23, 41, 46, 47, 49
Naval Air Station (NAS) **A12**, 26, 27, 30, 34, **35**, 36, 52
nuclear 10, 14, 26, 41
   strikes 5, 54; weapons **41**, 55

Operation *Rolling Thunder* 22, 39, 40, 43, 49
Operational Conversion Unit (OCU): 228 34, **52**, 53, 54, 55, **F56**
ordnance 6, 9, 10, 22, 23, **24**, 26, 27, **29**, 40, 46, 48, 49, 54, 61

quick-reaction alert (QRA) 32, **53**, 54, 55, 56, 58, 59

radars 4, 5, 6, 7, 8, 11, **12**, **16**, 17, 20, 24, 26, 27, 28, 29, 30, 31, 32, 36, 38, **40**, 41, **E44**, 47, 48, 53, 54, 55, 58, 59, 60, 61
   AN/AWG-10 **12**, 14, 15, 29, 35, 48; AN/APQ-50 5, **7**, 8; AN/APQ-72 8, 12, 40, **41**; radar homing and warning (RHAW) 12, 27, 41; radar intercept officer (RIO) 38, 40, **43**
reconnaissance **4**, 5, 6, 10, 11, 17, **B24**, 26, 27, 32, 40, 41, 43, 46, 50, 53, 54, 55, **F56**, 60
Rolls-Royce 14, **15**, 16, **21**, 30, 52
Royal Air Force (RAF), the 14, 15, 16, 17, 19, 23, **24**, 30, 31, **C32**, 34, **35**, **51**, **52**, 53, 54, 55, **F56**, 58, 60, 61
   Brüggen 51, 53, 54, **F56**; Germany (RAFG) 55, 58, 59; Leuchars **C32**, 51, 53, 54, 55, 56; No. 56 Sqn **16**, **26**, 55, 58; No. 892 Sqn **24**, **C32**, **51**, 52, 53; Phantom 53, 54, 58, **61**; Wattisham **52**, **53**, 55, 56, 58, **61**
Royal Naval Air Station (RNAS) Yeovilton 14, **15**, 16, 51, 53
Royal Navy, the 14, 15, 31, **C32**, 51, 54, 60
rudders **9**, 15, 19, 20, 61

Spiller, Wing Commander Nick **52**, **53**, 55, 58, 59, 61
stabilators **7**, 11, 12, 14, 16, **18**, 19, 27, 29, 31, 32, 34, 42, **50**

titanium 7, 16, 18, **20**

United States Marine Corps (USMC), the 9, 10, 12, 22, 23, 27, **29**, **34**, 35, **36**, 38, 39, 44, 46, 47, **48**, **49**, **50**, 51, 59, 60
US Navy, the 11, 36, 52
   USS *America* 29, 42, **E44**; USS *Coral Sea* **5**, 17, **D36**, 39, 40, 41, 44, 51; USS *Enterprise* **A12**, 41, 53; USS *Forrestal* **9**, 14, 36, 41, 51; USS *Franklin D. Roosevelt* 18–19, 41; USS *Independence* **36**, 40, 53; USS *Kitty Hawk* **28**, 29, 38, **41**; USS *Saratoga* 31, 36, 51, 52

USN fighter squadron (VF): VF-33 *Tarsiers* **A12**, 38, 39, 42, 43, **E44**; VF-41 *Black Aces* **34**, 40, 41, 42; VF-51 *Screaming Eagles* **34**, **39**, 44, 46; VF-84 *Jolly Rogers* **36**, 39, 40, 42; VF-92 *Silverkings* **A12**, 39, 46; VF-96 *Fighting Falcons* 29, 38, 39, 40, 41, 44, 46; VF-101 *Grim Reapers* 12, 26, 36; VF-102 *Diamondbacks* 27, 38, 42; VF-114 *Aardvarks* 22, 38, **41**, **43**; VF-121 *Pacemakers* 26, 38, 43; VF-142 *Ghostriders* 39, 42, 43; VF-151 *Vigilantes* **5**, **D36**, 39; VF-213 *Black Lions* **28**, 29, **40**

Vietnam 22, 34, 38, **39**, 46, 47, 48, 50, 60
   North 39, 47, 48, 49; South **4**, **A12**, 39, 41, 43, 49; War, the 9, 11, 12, 22, 23, **D36**, **49**

Westinghouse 4, 8, 12, 15, 41
World War II 23, 46, **53**